CISTERCIAN STUDIES SERIES:NUMBER ONE-HUNDRED AND FOUR

# WOMEN AND SAINT BERNARD OF CLAIRVAUX

by

Jean Leclercq

D0920672

CISTERCIAN STUDIES SERIES: NUMBER ONE-HUNDRED AND FOUR

# WOMEN AND SAINT BERNARD OF CLAIRVAUX

by
Jean Leclercq
Monk of Clervaux

Translated by
Marie-Bernard Saïd OSB

Cistercian Publications
Kalamazoo, Michigan
1989

A translation of *La femme et les femmes dans l'oeuvre de Saint Bernard*. Paris, Editions Pierre Tequi, 1982.

The work of Cistercian Publications is made possible in part by support from Western Michigan University to The Institute of Cistercian Studies

Available in Britain and Europe from
Cassells plc
Artillery House    Artillery Row
London    SW1P 1RT

Available elsewhere (including Canada) from
Cistercian Publications:Distribution
Saint Joseph's Abbey
Spencer, MA 01562

**Library of Congress Cataloguing-in-Publication**
Leclercq, Jean, 1911–
    [Femme et les femmes dans l'oeuvre de saint Bernard. English]
    Women and Saint Bernard of Clairvaux / by Jean Leclercq ;
translated by Marie-Bernard Said.
        p.   cm.   — (Cistercian studies series ; no. 104)
    Translation of: La femme et les femmes dans l'oeuvre de saint
Bernard.
    "Womankind and women in the works of Bernard of Clairvaux."
    Includes bibliographical references.
    ISBN 0-87907-604-6. — ISBN 0-87907-404-3 (pbk.)
    1. Bernard, of Clairvaux, Saint, 1090 or 91–1153—Views on women.
2. Women in Christianity—History.   3. Woman (Christian
theology)— History of doctrines—Middle Ages, 600–1500.   I. Title.
II. Title: Womankind and women in the works of Bernard of Clairvaux.
III. Series.
BV639.W7L41913   1989
271'.1202—dc20                                                          89-39159
                                                                                    CIP

*Printed in the United States of America.*

# TABLE OF
# CONTENTS

# INTRODUCTION

*O mulier...tua pulchritudo,*
*quae vere tua est...aeterna est*
*de aeternitate*

(SC 82.4)

S aint Bernard's personality, his work, and the role he played are too important, and his influence too profound, for us not to wonder what he thought about women, and what opinion he had of them. Surprisingly enough, we are, in this matter, still dependent on categorical and oversimplified statements.[1] The only way to avoid this state of affairs, which nowadays seems to have become traditional, is to study Saint Bernard's thought on the subject of women, not merely in a general sort of way, as has sometimes been done in brief but praiseworthy pages,[2] but in detail. Carefully avoiding foregone conclusions on abstract problems like 'the anthropology of women' or 'the theological concept of woman' in Saint Bernard's works, we must get down to examining, one after another, all the texts in which Bernard mentions women or addresses himself to them. Then we must study all the information, symbols, images, and ideas which we collect from these texts and put them into context, apart from which they

---

[1]Examples could be cited. A positive and well founded judgement has however been made by Edith Russel, 'Saint Bernard et les dames de son temps', in *Saint Bernard de Clairvaux* (Paris, 1953), 411–425.

[2]Just two pages in the synthesis made by Joan M Ferrante, *Women as Image in Medieval Literature from the Twelfth Century to Dante* (New York, 1975) 28–29.

cannot be correctly understood. We must also trace the sources on which they depend and the literary genre proper to each. And, of course, we must not forget to take into account the date of their composition, so far as this is known.

An enquiry of this kind is now possible because we have two good working tools: the recent critical edition of all Saint Bernard's works,[3] and the complete concordance which goes with it.[4] Only by analysis shall we avoid constructing facile syntheses, and discover whether or not there was a development in his thought. And if we notice Bernard taking different attitudes to women, does an examination of his psychology and his teaching enable us to discern several sides to his personality in this area? Are there, as it were, several different and successive Bernards? And if there are, how can they be reconciled with each other? Any description of the findings of such research will necessarily involve a certain amount of repetition. But this is a risk we must take if we want to avoid hasty generalizations which, over the long run, heedlessly are repeated. The works of Bernard will be examined, either singly or as a group, in chronological order.[5] Letters to women will be dealt with in a special chapter.

---

[3]*Sancti Bernardi Opera*, 8 volumes, Rome 1957–1977; cited henceforth as SBOp.

[4]Thesaurus Sancti Bernardi Claraevallensis, Corpus Christianorum (Turnhout: Brepols, 1988). I thank M.A.H. Martens, the main craftsman of this Concordance, who has never failed to facilitate my work at Bergeyk, Holland, and who untiringly answered my queries by letter. In all subsequent notes, as in this one, any references not preceded by the name of an author are publications in which I have dealt at greater length with subjects which can only be touched upon in the present book. One single exception will be the title *Bernard de Clairvaux* which refers to the book of the *Commission d'histoire de l'Ordre de Cîteaux* III (Paris: Alsatia, 1952).

[5]Notes giving references to the works of Saint Bernard will be set as follows: the divisions within each work (the book and/or paragraph number); the volume in which it occurs in the critical edition; the page in that volume and, when neccesary, the line. E.g. SC 74.4; II: 216,17–24 means Sermon 74 on the Song of Songs, paragraph 4; SBOp volume two, page 216, lines 17–24.

# CHAPTER I

# THE TEXTS

## 1. *Biblical Models in Bernard's First Works*

T HE EARLIEST DATED work of Saint Bernard in which he alludes to women is the treatise *On the Steps of Humility*, which was considered at Clairvaux as his 'first work'.[1] A first draft was circulated sometime in 1124, and resulted from sermons Bernard had preached to his monks. In it he mentions five women, all from the Bible, and this in itself is already characteristic. Bernard is speaking in this treatise, not of womankind in general, or of women about whom Scripture tells us almost nothing. The women Bernard mentions are models as well as historical figures, and they recur throughout his works.

First there is Dinah, the daughter of Jacob who was kidnapped during the imprudent outing we read about in Genesis (34:1–5) Traditionally the symbol of the heedless person, man or woman, who exposes self to sin,[2] in Bernard's writings she represents—with a preciseness which coincides exactly with the biblical sources—that curiosity

---

[1] *De gradibus humilitatis et superbiae* ( = *Hum*) in SBOp III; on the date, see SBOp III; 3–4.

[2] In *Monks and Love in Twelfth Century France* (Oxford, 1979) 59, nn. 47–50, I have cited and commented on some examples.

which he so often denounced as dangerous.[3] He speaks to her, but far from reproaching her, he questions her gently, neither hurting nor humiliating her (Hum 29; SBOp III:39, 7–14) Then he goes on to speak in the same way to Eve (30;39,15–40,9). These two women symbolize any human being who succumbs to sin's temptation.

A little further on in the treatise, we find two positive models, Martha and Mary. Bernard praises their faith and unswerving trust in Jesus: *O sanctae mulieres Christi familiares*. . . (52;55,14–56,11). Mary, the mother of the Lord, shows the same faith and trust (53; 56,12–26). We meet, then, in this very first work two types of feminine symbol: Martha, her sister Mary, and the Mother of Jesus, all three of whom are admired. Eve and Dinah are what we might call 'anti-models', but Bernard considers them more with compassion than with contempt.

Let us turn next to his collection of homilies on the Annunciation. The first draft of *Missus est* was published towards the end of 1124.[4] As we might foresee by the theme and the title, *In Praise of the Virgin Mother*, much more is said about Mary than about other women. The dignity lost by Eve is restored in Mary. This parallel between Eve and Mary provides the framework of the second homily in particular. Eve is inseparable from Adam and both are invited to rejoice and exult because—in one of those word plays Bernard so loved—they were not only *peremptores*, the sources of our ruin, but also *parentes*, parents of humankind (Miss II.3; SBOp IV:22,22–24). Their shame is taken away by a woman, the New Eve.

The Old Testament writers' emphatic insistence on the inferiority of woman, her congenital weakness, her bodily

---

[3]*'Curiositas* et le retour à Dieu chez S.Bernard', in *Divium. Homenaje a Manuel Diáz y Diáz* (Madrid, 1983) 133–141.

[4]SOBp IV; on the date, IV:3. The first redaction included only the first three homilies; in these, with one exception, we find the texts used here.

frailty, her 'slippery' mind, is all put right in Mary (II.5;24, 5–22), who is 'blessed among women'. We find this New Testament phrase repeated three times in the third homily (III.4;38,27;40,6; and II.11;28,21–22). In this way all earlier natural and spontaneous values are reversed. In Mary are accomplished the prophecies of Solomon concerning the valiant woman (Prov 31:30), the prophecy of Jeremiah fore-telling that a woman would encompass a man (Jer 31:22), and finally the prophecy of Isaiah who foresaw that a virgin would give birth to a child ([Is 7:14] II.11; 29,1–3).[5] Through Mary the original state of things is restored. Satan seduced woman before man. In Mary, Satan is overcome by a woman before being vanquished by Christ (II.13;30,–14–21). In the fourth homily, a later addition to the first three, Bernard applies to Mary the praise which the Bridegroom of the Song of Songs sings to his lady love: 'O thou who are more beautiful than all other women' ([Sg 1:7] IV.8;54,3).

Three other treatises may be related to this early period of Bernard's literary career. In the book *De diligendo Deo*, composed after 1126,[6] only two women are mentioned: the Church and the Samaritan woman. The Church is the bride of the true Solomon, greatly to be admired, and to her we may apply the words of the Song (Dil 7; SBOp III:124, 17–26). Jesus spoke to the Samaritan at Jacob's well. Ber-nard mentions her briefly and proposes her as an 'exam-ple' for all humans (26;141,5–12). In the treatise *On Grace and Free Choice*, composed before or around 1128,[7] the Wis-dom of God is likened to the woman in the Gospel who swept her house to find a lost coin. God seeks his own image among humankind and this 'evangelical woman' provides a wonderful image of God's care for his creature (Gra 31; SBOp III:188,22–28). Finally, in the treatise *On*

---

[5] Cp. his interpretation of the same prophets in the sermon *In purifica-tione* 3,1; IV:341,24–342,4.

[6] SBOp III; on the date, p. 111.

[7] *Ibid.*, on the date, 157.

*Precept and Dispensation,* written before 1143–1144[8] Gomer, the adulteress—*mulier fornicatoria*—with whom the prophet Hosea coupled at God's request, is excused simply because of this divine command (Pre 6; SBOp III:258,2–9). Here, as in all the other texts we have quoted, what Bernard considers is not the historical event, the person referred to by the letter of Scripture, but the meaning. The wisdom books and christian authors from Jerome to the end of the Middle Ages saw in woman only her nature and her character. Bernard chose to see her role, and in every case this is positive, because of Christ.

## 2. *Images in His Two Final Works*

In what he wrote, did Bernard develop in this point from what he wrote in his youthful days to the works of his old age? We have two works dating from the last years of his life. Let us examine them.

*The Life of Saint Malachy,* archbishop of Armagh in Ireland, was written sometime between Malachy's death at Clairvaux on the second or third of November, 1148, and Bernard's own death in 1153.[9] In it, as is customary in the genre of hagiography, real women offer a pretext for evoking biblical models. Even so, this is rare. In his youth, Malachy, like some new Tobias, was 'tempted by a woman, or more exactly, through the intermediary of a woman, he is tempted by the serpent', that is to say, by the devil on whom the fault then falls. The woman reproaches Malachy each day for his good works in burying the dead. He opposes non-violence to the 'silliness of this foolish woman' who was a kinswoman (V.Mal. 3; SBOp III:314, 19–25). Later, a 'wretched woman' possessed by the devil interrupts his preaching, insults him, and reproaches him for his baldness. But Malachy, a new Elijah, answers nothing, and God himself punishes her (29;337,13–22). His

---

[8]*Ibid.,* on the date, 244–245.
[9]*Ibid.,* on the date, 297.

own sister, whom he rebuked for living according to the flesh and who had consequently broken off relations with him, dies, and Malachy prays for her, obtaining God's forgiveness for her (11;320,4–25)—one more example of a woman's misconduct ending up as a cause for edification.

But more importantly, Malachy exerted his power to do good for many women. He heals a dumb woman, a raving madwoman, a paralytic; he protects another from a demon while she spends the night in prayer (40–41;246,5–247,8); he delivers not one but two possessed women (45;350, 14–22), restores speech to another mute (46;352,1–4 and 47;352,5–8). He even causes a pregnant woman who had been unable to deliver to give birth. She was 'a good and virtuous woman' whom everyone recommended to him (47;352,15–28). He avenges a woman victimized by an incestuous count (48;353,7–26). He calms a furiously angry woman who becomes a model of gentleness (54;358,5–23). It was to a woman that God revealed that Malachy would again make prosperous again an island sinking into poverty and becoming depopulated; fish were no longer being caught there, but thanks to Malachy shoals of them came back (55;359,4–20). Finally, the last miracle Malachy performed was to give beauty back to a girl disfigured by cancer (69;373,15–18). The number and nature of the benefits this saint bestowed on women surprise us. And this was a man for whom Saint Bernard had great admiration.

We come at length to the last treatise Bernard wrote *On Consideration*, composed at the very end of his life for the edification of Pope Eugene III.[10] The subject hardly lent itself to talk about women. At the beginning Bernard compared himself to a very tender and somewhat possessive woman in his relationship with the recipient, the pope who had been a monk of his own Order (Csi, praef.; SBOp III:393–94).[11] Then, listing the various categories of the

---

[10]*Ibid.*, on the date, 381.

[11]See *Nouveau visage de saint Bernard. Approches psycho-historiques* (Paris, 1976) 51 [ET forthcoming as *A Second Look at Saint Bernard*].

faithful who came under the pope's pastoral care, Bernard carefully mentions that women count as much as men (1.6;400,10). Further on we come across an allusion out of tune with the rest. Bernard speaks of 'man born of woman and therefore guilty'(II.18;426,6). Sure enough, the first words are a reminiscence of Job(5:7) and the next are all part of a phrase in which all elements share the same ending: *reatu, metu, fletu.* Is it possible that Bernard fell victim to his own talent? Were his harsh words about woman a result of his attempt to complete his word play, to use the literary trick of paranomasia?[12] This impression is balanced towards the end of the treatise by an admirable parallel between the woman who put leaven into the flour and Mary in whose body the Word united with human nature (V.22;484,24–485,2). Bernard uses the same comparison elsewhere, saying 'Blessed is the woman in whom this happened'(Nat 2.24.iv; SBOp IV:254,12–16).

## 3. *Real Women in Bernard's Letters*

In Bernard's some five hundred extant letters, he speaks of women only fourteen times when writing to men, and then by way of allusion.[13] On the other hand, he sent out twenty-three letters to women, some of them quite lengthy. These two groups of letters must be examined separately. The first tell us what Bernard thought of women. The second reveal his personal attitude towards women of various categories and demonstrate how his reactions varied from one group or person to another.

We can draw little from Bernard's letters to men. And the best way for us to find out what little there is is to go through his register in chronological order, as it was

---

[12] The importance of word play in S. Bernard has been examined by Dorette Sabersky-Bascho, *Studien zur Paronomasie bei Bernard von Clairvaux* (Fribourg, Switzerland, 1979).

[13] SBOp VII–VIII.

assembled either by himself or under his orders.[14] It should, however, be pointed out that the earliest of those letters which have come down to us sets the tone, so to speak, for all the other letters in which he speaks of women who really did play some part in his life. This letter did not find its way into the register because it concerned Bernard's own person rather than the message he wished to hand on in the collection of published letters. The letter in question dates from the beginning of his abbacy. Physically exhausted by the hard work of founding Clairvaux, he was taking a rest cure at the request and under the jurisdiction of the bishop of Châlons, William of Champeaux. In a message sent to his prior at Clairvaux, Bernard says that, at the intervention of a noble lady, Beatrice of Ville-sous-la-Ferté, he has obtained the bishop's permission to spend the winter nearer his community, at Clémintinpré, a grange belonging to the benedictine abbey of Saint-Bénigne at Dijon (Ep 441; SBOp VIII:419).[15] This brief mention shows us something about the good relations he kept up, even in those early days, with Beatrice, to whom he was later to write. But more particularly, the letter shows how much influence a laywoman could exercise on Bernard's behalf with a churchman as conscious of his authority as William of Champeaux.

One of the earliest letters in the register is also one of the most touching. This is letter 39, written towards the end of 1127. In it Bernard commends several matters to count Thibaut of Champagne. After having pleaded on behalf of the Canons Regular of Larzicourt, Bernard goes on to say, 'Here is another thing I earnestly ask of you. As I was going through Bar recently, a poor woman, overcome with

---

[14] On the nature of the collection of Saint Bernard's letters, see 'Recherches sur la collection des épîtres de saint Bernard', in *Cahiers de civilisation médiévale* 14 (1971) 205–219; 'Lettres de saint Bernard: histoire ou littérature?' in *Studi Medievali* 12 (1971) 1–74.

[15] On this text, Damien van den Eynde, 'Les premiers écrits de saint Bernard', in *Recueil d'études sur saint Bernard*, III (Rome, 1969) 357–360.

grief, came to see me. What she told me of her sorrows so upset me that I cannot help pleading for her with you. She is the wife of that fellow Belin whom you were obliged to punish severely some time ago for a crime he had committed. Please have pity on this woman, and God will have pity on you' (Ep 39.2; VII:98,7–12).

At the same period, in 1127 or 1128, Bernard wrote to Henry, called the Boar, archbishop of Sens, the long letter 42 which is a veritable treatise *On the Conduct and Duties of Bishops.* Here, too, before defending the poor and denouncing prelatial pomp, Bernard warns his correspondent that he will need courage. What model does he propose in the very first sentence? The valiant woman of Proverbs (31:19). On the other hand, when he wants to caricature the ridiculous and costly elegance of bishops, he quotes a warning given by Saint Paul to the 'weaker sex': 'No costly attire (1 Tim 2:9). . . Let us leave these frills and flounces to women. They have nothing but worldly affairs in their heads and are anxious to please their husbands. Hence their habitual concern with what to wear. But as for you, priest of the most high God, whom do you seek to please?' (4–5;104, 4–21). Notice that Bernard recognizes how legitimate this elegance is for women seeking to please their husbands, for this is one of the forms of marital love. Not long afterwards, somewhere between 1128 and 1136, in his *Praise of the New Knighthood, to the Knights of the Temple,* when he mocked the complicated, affected and cumbersome clothing of worldly knights, Bernard says that they too follow feminine fashions: *ritu femineo.*[16] And he describes it in the same way he did when writing about bishops: long hair falling over their eyes preventing them from seeing, bouffant shirts, sleeves flopping about all over the place. Bernard has nothing against such 'adorn-

---

[16] The word *ritus* used here had, already in antiquity, the sense of *mos, consuetudo,* and, in the ablative, the sense of 'after the fashion of', of *more, modo,* according to E. Ernout-A. Meillet, *Dictionnaire étymologique de la langue latine. Histoire des mots* (Paris, 1932) 827.

ments'; he merely says that they are meant for maidens, not for military men; *militaria sunt. . .an muliebria*? (Tpl 3; III:216,11–18). Let the bishop, then, practice humility, and not be like those two creatures who, because of their pride, envied God—that is, the devil who envied his power, and woman who envied his knowledge (an allusion to the hope that Eve nurtured when the demon told her 'You shall be like gods') (Ep 42.18; 114:15–19). When, in 1131, Hildebert, archbishop of Tours, was stubbornly upholding the anti-pope Pierleone, Bernard compared him harshly to the foolish virgins of the gospel parable: 'I am ashamed, I must say, to see that the ancient serpent has, by new daring, left these foolish women to try to undermine the very strength of your heart. . .'(124; VII:304,3–8). Here we see an unfavorable biblical formula applied to a prelate. There is no doubt about it, on the rare occasions when Bernard speaks negatively about women, he always applies it to men.

In his letters, except when he was writing about real women, Bernard made quite a lot of use of feminine biblical symbols. In his letter to his young cousin Robert, whom he considered a deserter from Cîteaux to Cluny, he says that he is both father and mother to Robert: 'I fed you with my milk. . .'. And now, 'the same thing has happened to me as happened to the harlot in Solomon's day, she whose child was kidnapped by another woman. You too have been snatched away from my breast. . . .I cannot forget the child of my bosom' (Ep 1.10; VII:8,8–18). Both these comparisons are complimentary to women. Again, in the letter where Bernard asks Aelred of Rievaulx to write the work called *The Mirror of Charity*, he refutes Aelred's objection that the burden is too heavy for his frail feminine shoulders (523; VII:486,13–16).

So much for the few images and ideas about women in letters to men. Next we find a few practical warnings intended for those women and men who had become monks and nuns. The archbishop of Trier, Adalbero, was admonished to see to it that there is no abuse—fornication or anything else—among the nuns of Saint-Maur's, Verdun. In several instances Bernard opposes allowing women into monasteries of monks. There are allusions to this in connection with Saint Denis, about 1127 (78.4; VII:203,22–23), and Aulps in 1134 (254.1; VII:156,16). He always warned against women and monks living together, a practice 'rightly to be feared', as experience had proven. Bernard issued this warning after a monk of Cusset had committed a shameful fault. The responsibility lay, not with the woman, but with the monk and his abbot. Bernard asks that the monk be treated with indulgence and prudence and that he be allowed to remain in religious life. The 'crime' he had committed was certainly not one of the most serious (79.1–2;210–212). We shall have opportunity to come back to the last part of this letter later, in connection with women frequenting a monastic mill.

Two letters have given rise to conjectures among historians because the woman concerned, Petronilla, abbess of Fontevrault, is named only in the first of them (200; VIII:57–59), and because the second does no more than make a passing allusion to the conflict she had with Ulger, bishop of Angers (340; VIII:281). The bishop and the abbess were at odds over bridges on the river Loire over which she had rights. In a first message, sent to Ulger, Bernard defended the abbess with a vigor that led him to speak to this powerful and severe bishop with an amazing vivacity, not to say, violence. Bernard tells him outright that neither his name nor his title, nor his venerable age, gives him the right to be unjust to Petronilla. Later, however, it seems Bernard asked Innocent III to be kind to this aged prelate. In Bernard's view, what opposed bishop and abbess was less bridges than the contrast between the prelate and the representative of a modern form of monasticism born of the eremitical life,[17] as Fontevrault and Cîteaux were.

---

[17] J-M. Bienvenu, 'Le conflit entre Ulger, évêque d'Angers, et Pétronille de Chemillé, abbesse de Fontevrault (vers 1140–1149)', in *Revue Mabillon*, 58 (1970–1975) 132.

'Furthermore, Ulger, a follower of the misogynist Marbode (d. 1123), did not perhaps demonstrate an overwhelming sympathy for the abbess, a strong-willed woman who commanded not only nuns, but brothers, too'.[18] Bernard did not share the bishop's antipathy.

Some of his letters Bernard considered less important than those he collected together in his register. They are none-the-less authentic and in matters dealing with women ring as true as those in the register. When another occasion arose for him to warn religious about keeping company with women, he laid the blame, not on the women, but on the men who exposed themselves to danger. He wrote to a male recluse to whom he had forbidden visits from, or conversation with, women, and advised that, if this were impossible for him, he should give up the solitary life, which no one was forcing him to lead (404; VIII:385). Of a certain bishop Leontius, whose scandalous life Bernard denounced on several points, he asks—without however gliding from suspicion to judgement and condemnation—'Tell me now, I pray you, to be constantly with a woman and not to know her, is that not something more difficult than raising the dead? You cannot do easier things and you expect people to think you can do this? To be at table every day with a girl in your room, to talk to her while looking her in the eyes, to hold hands with her while at work. You do all that, and you expect to be considered as living continently? Maybe you are. But as for me, I am a little suspicious. It scandalizes me. Do away with this cause of scandal. If you do not want to scandalize the Church, send this woman away' (538; VIII:505,5–11). Once more it is the man, the bishop, and not his companion who is denounced. In echoing the tradition of the Church on the way bishops and monks should live, Bernard was well aware of his own frailty. But not a word is said about that of women.

---

[18] *Ibid.*, 122–123.

One letter (415; VIII:399) contrasts in style and tone with the others. It is written to an unnamed young man who had committed himself by a 'promise', even by a contract, a 'pact', to entering Clairvaux. But he did not arrive and Bernard finally discovered why: the same reason that 'defeated the ever courageous David and led a very wise Solomon into error'. 'He is enchained by a fatal fetter on his foot' which is holding him in miserable captivity. Bernard urged the lad to set himself free from this 'cruel beast' —words which are applied to the devil in the account of the death of Saint Martin and which we find in an antiphon drawn from this Life, hagiographical and liturgical texts everyone knew. These biblical and monastic allusions prove just how indignant Bernard was to think that a postulant for Clairvaux was having what he called an 'affair' or, as we would say, was tied down.

In short, then, when everything is put into its right perspective, we see that in his letter collection Bernard has little to say about women and practically nothing about womankind. Clearly he was neither obsessed with them nor pessimistic. He was careful not to discredit them when writing to men towards whom he shows great severity. Was he severe when writing to women? We shall see about this by looking at his letters to women in the next chapter.

## 4. *Bernard Speaking to his Monks.*

We now know that Bernard's great sermons on the christian mysteries, his theological commentary of the liturgical year, were not delivered as they were dictated and then arranged by Bernard himself into a complete synthesis. We shall have to examine this type of literature by itself later. But even so we may take a look at those sermons which are called 'diverse' or 'short' or even, sometimes, 'sentences'. They are more likely to give us a true echo of what Bernard actually did say to his monks, some of whom took notes. These sermons are to be found in the two tomes of Volume Six of the critical edition of his works.[19]

Contrary to the great doctrinal texts, these shorter sermons generally have a practical purpose. One of the problems which led Bernard to speak of women was temptation. This is part of a monk's life, as it is part of the life of any other christian, and Bernard liked to deal with it by referring to the first temptation in the Bible, in which Eve played a major part. According to Genesis (3:8) it is undeniable that 'man gave in to woman when she suggested disobedience' (*Varii, De vii domis*, I; VI/1:45,4). Any misogyny there may be in this remark comes from Scripture. But in other places where Bernard mentions this same event, he either makes the man as responsible as the woman, or else he lays the greater blame on Adam. Even though it was the woman who proffered the forbidden fruit, the man was free to accept or to refuse and consequently he takes full responsibility for his consent to sin. In Latin a play on words highlights the idea: Eve only offered, there was no violence, *offerendo. . . non violentiam inferendo.* And Bernard, addressing himself to Adam says, 'It was not by her power, but by your will—*potestate, voluntate*—that you obeyed her voice rather than God's. She led you into error, but she neither pushed nor forced you'. This is very accurate theology and Bernard goes on to apply it to every person who commits sin knowingly (Div 11.2; VI/1:125,10–13). He harkens back several times to the fact that Eve made the 'suggestion', but Adam gave his 'consent' (Sent III.107; VI/2:174,12). And, what is more, Adam's sin was the more grievous because he shunted all the responsibility on to Eve, whereas it was he who was to blame (Div 102.1; VI/1:369–9–11). In Adam the sin was consummated even though it began with Eve, who is a symbol of character

---

[19] SBOp VI/volumes 1 and 2 contain *Sermones varii* (*Varii*); *De diversis* (*D*); *Sententiarum* (*S*) series I,II,III; *Parabolae* (*Par*).

weakness: *Mulieres, id est illos molles, qui Evae conforman-tur...* ' (Sent III.110; VI/2:187,16). In reminding us of temptation, Bernard sometimes reminds us of the Tempter, too (Div 22,3; VI/1:172,1–19). In short, the serpent showed malice, woman only ignorance — *malitiam, ignorantiam* — (Div 49; VI/1:269,5).

Bernard took up these ideas again, enlarging on them and enriching them with psychological considerations, in a sermon where he explains that, 'Woman led man into sin, and she ought to have wept over her sin rather than aggravate it by adding another to it. But she felt she would find some consolation if she could persuade man to share her sin. It is natural enough that a person should wish to have a companion either in sin or in virtue. . . . She sinned through ignorance, but Adam, who consented, through weakness. He sinned by undue love for his wife, not because he did his wife's will, but because he preferred it to God's will. . . . To his wife he was bound by love alone, but to God he was bound by fear and love.' Adam's behavior is explained by his marital love: *erga coniugis affectum. . . , cuius amore peccavit.* But this love was inordinate, unconformed to the law of God. To that first sin Adam added another by blaming his own sin on his wife: not only did he make excuses for himself, but he went so far as to accuse Eve, and in this way he became even guiltier than she. Yet she in turn did the same thing by throwing blame on the serpent. She too was endowed with freedom, and she should have been able to resist the serpent's suggestion, but through pride, she gave in to temptation. Although she is far from being alone in this original sin, she did nevertheless bear her share of responsibility. But these faults, like every other fault, have all been put right through the coming of Christ (Div 66.1–3; VI/1:300–301). At the annunciation, Mary talked to God through the intermediary of an angel and she showed she had all the virtues which were lacking in Adam and Eve: courage, humility, prudence, sincerity (Div 52.3–4; VI/1:276).

Mary and Eve are contrasted, briefly and in passing, in a Sentence to which a copyist added the words 'It is the devil who harmed Eve' (Sent III.87; VI/1:127,9). We do, however, find a curious text in which Bernard twice attributes to a monk the expression 'My Eve' in speaking of what is fleshly in every human person: the flesh has been given to the mind as Eve to Adam, to be a helpmate and so that together they may beget children, that is, good actions. . . . The serpent, crept up to the ear of my Eve and poured in the venom of evil suggestion'. He led her to the forbidden fruit, she came back with him and 'put the fruit of disobedience into the mouth' of Adam while he was asleep. He ate it and discovered he was 'entirely fleshly' (Par VIII; VI/2:299). Elsewhere, Bernard says that any human being must love the Eve within himself and live in peace with her. In such texts, Eve is no more than a symbol for the whole human race.

We find the same thing with other biblical models, examples to be avoided. These Bernard mentions briefly: Dinah, who fell victim to her curiosity and its consequences, as can befall every 'soul', man or woman (Sent III.89; VI/2:137, 2–3;98, 161, 18–20); Michal who in her pride mocked David (Div 41.6; VI/1; 248,25); Delilah, who tore out Samson's eyes; Jezebel who murdered Naboth; Herodias who had John the Baptist beheaded (Sent II.117; VI/2:46).

Yet the women most often mentioned are those to be imitated, and here, as elsewhere, Bernard took his examples from the New Testament rather than the Old, and, in fact, restricted himself to the Gospels. In the Old Testament there are, of course, women such as the widow of Sarepta who fed Elijah (1 K 17:8–16; Sent II.122; VI/2;47,14); Abigail, the young Sunamite woman who warmed David 'without making him burn' (Sent III.88; VI/2;130,16); the Ethiopian woman who gave good advice to Naaman (*ibid.* p.130,18–131,3); and 'the seven women who took hold of one man', mentioned by Isaiah (4:1 and 11:1–3) and who were to become symbols of the gifts of the Holy Spirit (Sent

III.126; VI/2:245,21): they could hardly have a more honorable interpretation given them, or a more amusing one. Those listening to Bernard must surely have smiled! In the New Testament the woman with an issue of blood is healed by Jesus and then defended by him (Div 25.2:VI/1:188,12). Bernard gives her special praise in five different passages: (Div 96[VI/1:358, 13–23]; 99 [366,9]; 107.1:379,13]; S II.87 [ VI/2:42,4–5]; Sent III.101;[VI/2,168,30]). The Canaanite congratulated by Jesus because of her great faith (Div 107.1; VI/1:379,19–380,1 and Ep 512.1; VIII:395,8–11), and the 'holy women' at Christ's sepulchre are the image of the good things we receive from God by the mind, the hand, and the tongue (Div 58.1; VI/1:288,1–11)— another entertaining interpretation! The gifts of the Holy Spirit were given first to women and then to men, for Christ appeared to them only after having shown himself to women (Sent I.27; VI/2:16, 19). And Mary is, of course, the perfect woman because she is both a virgin and a mother, chaste yet fruitful (Sent III.87; VI/2:128,1–11). To sum up: in the Gospels, Bernard found only admirable women.

Had he anything to say to his monks about the nature and the role of woman? A little, but he was not particularly interested in the question. He does mention in passing— following Saint Paul to the Colossians (3:11)—the theological basis of the equal dignity of men and women: with God there is no distinction of persons; anyone who fears God and does what is right in his eyes is acceptable to him (Sent III.127; VI/2;249,15). There is also a passing allusion to Job's wife, who says silly things to her husband; his children (Job 2:10) are set in contrast with prelates who, if they have charity, love and form their subjects (Sent III.121; VI/2: 226–227). Women, before they come to marriageable age, appear weak and feeble, and they are then the symbol of those who have not yet reached the full stature of manhood. But in the Gospel the Lord defends Magdalene, a 'delicate soul'; she is still a woman, a tender creature, as yet unable to fulfill great charges. But—and this is a symbolism applicable to all, men and women alike—she will grow from woman to manhood, that is, she will come to full spiritual maturity (Div 90.3; VI/1:339,2–4). In the same way the abandoned little girl who, according to Ezekiel, God took to himself, bathing her, perfuming her, and clothing her in fine raiment, is like a bride on whom the bridegroom showers gifts to make her worthy of becoming his wife. This is what God does with the Synagogue and especially with Mary, now raised above men and angels (Sent III.111; VI/2:189,9–16).

As we can see, these are considerations of an elevated nature. When talking to his monks, Bernard did not rant about women in any way, nor did he warn them to be on their guard against the danger women presented. He tended rather to show women in a favorable light, sometimes very charmingly but without either exaggeration or prejudice. And without the clumsiness of Abelard in treating the history of feminine monasticism.[20] Bernard's balance is to be explained by the fact that he always followed the gospel narratives; he was no more a misogynist than the Lord was.

## 5. *Theological Reflections in the Sermons*

Among the major sermons carefully written for publication, we find one outstanding exception in matters touching women. This is the text *On Conversion, to Clerics*, a sermon originally preached to students at Paris, probably between Lent 1139 and the beginning of 1140.[21] We know nothing about the sermon itself, but Bernard later set down in writing a first short draft in which he reused and developed somewhat one of his sermons for All Saints Day. Then, he made it all into a longer text which took on the appearance of a real treatise. Having in mind an audience

---

[20] Abelard, Ep 7; *PL* 178:225–256; 'Le témoignage monastique d'Abelard', in *Revue d'ascétique et de mystique* 45 (1970) 168–172.
[21] SBOp IV:61.

of secular ecclesiastical students, some of whom prided themselves on knowing the ancient classical authors, Bernard adopted a style designed to please and convince them. *De conversione* is the only one of his works to use reminiscences of this kind. About ten of them have been identified.[22] This is particularly true of the passage in which he likens the human will given up to natural drives to 'a furious old hag' (*vetula furens*). In the portrait he sketches, which could hardly be more ridiculous, he describes her with 'hair standing on end, all over the place'— phrases found in Ovid.[23] She lashes out at reason and describes herself as 'inquisitive, passionate, and ambitious, rebellious in every way' (Conv VI.10), yet even so she is united to reason as in marriage. She winds up her diatribe with words from the *Thebaïs* of Statius: 'Retreating in indignation and fury, she says, "I have you in my clutches and I'll hold you a long time"'.[24] That is the only detailed description Bernard ever gave of a woman, and it is imaginary. But notice that it applies not to any particular woman, not to womankind, but to the will of every human being.

And what about those sermons where Bernard deals with his most cherished theme, the mystery of salvation and the part the human person plays in it? This indeed is the theme which lies at the heart of the theological summa made up by the liturgical sermons. Here again, underlying everything, is the first sin and the two people who committed it—both Adam and Eve, not Eve alone. 'It was woman's ignorance which blinded us (*excaecaverat nos*)' is followed immediately by another, not at all lenient, statement on man: 'Led astray, lured by his own concupiscence, he drained us of our energy (*enervaverat nos*)' (Pur 1.3; IV:336,18–19). Sometimes Bernard is equally hard on

---

[22]*Recueil d'études sur saint Bernard* . . . , III (Rome, 1969) 70.

[23]Parallel texts of Ovid are quoted in *Bernard de Clairvaux*, 553.

[24]Conv 10; IV:82–84; Statius, *Thebaïs*, II,429; *Bernard de Clairvaux*, 553.

both Adam and Eve: 'Together a man and a woman did us harm' (O Assumpt 1; V:262,1). Occasionally—and more often—he is more severe on Adam: 'Being the head of woman, as Saint Paul says [Eph 5:23], and since she was inferior to him, he ought to have shown her compassion and discipline' (OS 1.11; V:336,222). Then, when she had given in to the Tempter, Adam ought to have excused her, saying to God, 'Lord, the woman, being weaker, let herself be seduced; but it is I who have done wrong, it is I who have committed the sin'. But Adam does not do this and Bernard goes on to reproach him strongly for his wickedness (OS 1.12;338). Woman's ignorance is no better than man's softness, except that softness is a sort of weakness generally attributed to women (Pur 1.3; IV:336,18). In only one instance, and then in passing and without emphasis, Bernard seems to attribute to woman alone the eruption of death into human destiny: 'death, cruel and foolish, came from the falseness of the ancient serpent and woman's lack of wisdom' (Trans Mal 3; V:419,18–19). But elsewhere Bernard excuses Eve and lays the blame on Adam: 'The woman was easily seduced. But man was not seduced, he was simply bowled over by love for the woman' (Adv 1.9; V:443,6–8). It is, however, interesting to note here again that the reason for Adam's downfall was love for his wife— which is quite legitimate as long as it is rightly ordered.

The remedy for this first sin came through Mary: 'In her the curse which came through Eve is changed' (VNat 444.3; IV:223,16). Neither the idea nor the formula are unique to Bernard. Elsewhere he says 'She alone among women was set free from the common curse and the pains of childbirth' (O Assumpt 9; V:269,9–10). There is no point in dwelling on this aspect of Bernard's mariology. It has nothing original about it but follows a long tradition. One more text is worth looking at. In it Bernard stresses that 'Faithful Mary poured out the anti- venom serum to both men and women', who are thus, from a theological point of view, put on equal footing (*ibid.*,2;p.263,6–7). Solomon, in despair and wonderment, asked, 'Who shall find a valiant woman?' (Prov 31:10). But according to Bernard, his wonderment does not concern only women, for there have never been more than a few just persons. According to Genesis (7:7) and Saint Peter (1 P 3:20), there were only eight, before the flood (Nat BMV 4; V:277,16- 21).

What then is Bernard's opinion of women? In all his liturgical sermons—two whole volumes of the critical edition—there is only one unfavorable judgement. In describing the misery of the human condition—inspired by the Books of Ecclesiasticus and Job—Bernard commenting on what Job, says, 'Nothing is more abject than man born of woman'. We may wonder whether these words and those that follow concern man's historical condition, his nature and the existence of two sexes, or the religious situation of humanity in God's presence. An interpretation of this last sort is suggested by the image of the Man who saved mankind from so wretched a state: 'He too was born of a Virgin, and even more, formed from a woman'; as Saint Paul wrote to the Galatians (4:4), *factus ex muliere* (IV HM; V:60,20–21). When he mentions human nature itself and the physical weakness of women and children'who can attend combat but cannot fight', Bernard is simply remarking on a universally true fact, not comparing the sexes (Clem 4; V:415,10–11). On the other hand, when talking about the vanity which drives human beings to wear squirrel and ermine skins destined for 'worms and mice', men and women are lumped together: 'It is unworthy of men and forbidden for women; everyone, man or woman, shames rather than adorns himself'(I Nov 2.2; V:308,17–19).

Lastly, it is no surprise to find that Bernard, in these liturgical sermons, as in all his works, is full of praise for women who were 'devoted' (Pasc 1.5; V:80) or 'holy' (Pasc 2.3; V:96,17 and 3.6;109,7–8), those 'few' who had the courage to follow Christ on the way of the cross (Pasc 2.4;97,5). Elizabeth is called 'holy' (JB 4; V:179,8), and Mary of course is 'blessed' (Asspt 2.2; V:232,2,14–15). Martha and Mary are often praised in his sermons for the Assumption. These two women refute Solomon's words, 'Better is the wickedness of a man than a woman doing good' (Qo 42:14), because both performed an excellent work, one in serving the Lord, the other in listening to him (Asspt 3.3:240–241). In short, there is no systematic demeaning of women by comparison with men. In affirming their equality before God, Bernard never hesitated to complete a sentence in the Bible: 'If I wanted to magnify the mercies of God', Solomon wrote, 'behold some men of mercy' (Si 44:10). Bernard hastened to add 'and some women too' (Asspt 4.5; V:248, 10–11). This addition to a text of Scripture suggests a deliberate intention of rectifying an omission.

### 6. *Womankind and Human Destiny in the Sermons on the Song of Songs*

The series of eighty-six sermons on the beginning of the Song of Songs which Bernard dictated between 1135 and the year of his death is his masterpiece in the sense that, in them, once he himself had attained full spiritual and literary maturity, he dealt with the important problems which assail every christian conscience in every epoch as well as with those peculiar to his own age.[25] He did this in the form of sermons which, taken individually or in groups, constitute a series of deeply theological treatises. It would have been impossible to leave out the mystery of womankind.

True to tradition, Bernard quotes Genesis 1:27, which affirms the equality of man and woman, both created in the image of God (66.4; II:180,30–31). Physically, woman is weaker than man, who symbolizes the strength of the adult, which then applies by analogy to the role of bishops within the Church. But woman symbolizes those faithful in the Church who play a less active but no less necessary and

---

[25] SBOp, vols I-II; on the chronology, xv-xvi; on the nature of the work, *Recueil d'études sur saint Bernard . . .*, I (Rome, 1962) 193–212.

elevated role: the contemplatives (12.8–9; I:65–66). Yet still more profoundly, by reason of her innate frailty woman symbolizes all that is physical and earthly, in contrast with the heavenly choirs who represent all that is fully spiritual. This frailty is characteristic of 'secular souls', all those men and women who lack constancy and energy and whose whole life and every activity betray a sort of softness (38.4: II:16–17). But above all, this feminine frailty is the image of the physical, earthly condition of every human person, it is the symbol of everything in us that is unfinished, partial (*ex parte*) even though we are already saved. For this reason it behooves a Christian to avoid all curiosity and remain humble (38.5; II:17–18). For Bernard, feminine frailty is considered, not in itself, as some mere biological fact, but as a symbol and in comparison with the final perfection yet to come (45.3; II:51–52).

On the other hand, women have unique qualities: their capability for motherly love, for example. Even the poorest woman refuses to abandon her child to accept the invitation to a rich man's banquet (12,4; I:63,1–5). Among woman's virtues, Bernard twice mentions devotedness which, when shown towards Christ, becomes devoutness (12.7; I:65, 6 and 23.9; I:145, 4–5). Bernard knew that 'a wife is the glory of her husband' as Joseph proved when he resisted the solicitations of the wife of Potiphar (13.4; I:70,27–71,6). What can be said about women's capability for giving birth? Bernard sees in this privilege a model, not only for himself, but for all who contribute to the birth of Christ in souls (29.6; I:207,13–17).

Women have their place in the history of salvation. When God wanted to reveal himself to humankind, he sent angels'not only to some very spiritual men, but also to lowly persons, and even to women' (54.2; II:103,28–104,2). 'Joshua, Jethro, Gideon, and Samson all gloriously triumphed over God's enemies. But so did Judith, even though she was a woman' (13.5; I:71,21–22). In the prophet Jeremiah (3:31) we read of a brazen prostitute who represents despair, the refusal to repent (42.4; II:35,5–7), and this can be applied to the proud pharisee, to Judas and to many others. But in the same prophet (3:1) an adulterous woman is invited to return to her husband, and becomes the symbol of reconciliation between God and his chosen people (84.7; II:306,20–24).

The Gospel is full of praise for the canaanite woman. She is a model of faith for the whole Church (66.10; II:184, 19–21). In Martha and Mary timidity is natural and devotion the working of grace (71.4; II:216,18–25). After the resurrection, Mary Magdalene becomes a woman who no longer judges according to the flesh, but can now touch her Lord with'the hand of faith,''the finger of desire, the embrace of devotion, the eye of the spirit' (28.8–10; I:197–199). And addressing at some length the women who buried Christ, Bernard says'Oh! you good women' (75.8; II:251, 19). Finally, there is the Virgin Mary, who bore within herself'the majesty of the Word, carrying his inaccessible light' (31.9; I:225,20–22). When Jesus was twelve years old, he left the Temple, his Father's house, and'the Word and the Wisdom of God obeyed a carpenter and a woman' (19.7; SBOp I:113,3–6). Was he not formed in this same woman? (Gal 4:4,SC 53.8; II:101,4). When he ascended into heaven, she was there praying with his disciples, men and women together (42.11; II:40,5–9).

Despite his respect for women, Bernard knew that sin was not unknown to them. When he reproved the Rhineland heretics, he included women as well as men, though he was more lenient towards them (65.7; II:176,21–30). He held the men responsible for deviations, because they were the guardians of social order (66.14; II:187,19–29). Woman did have a share in the fault of the first man (16.11; I:95,29–30). When she trusted a serpent, she behaved like a woman devoid of wisdom (69.2,II:203,17); she was tricked by the serpent's guile (85.8; II:312,28–30). Consequently, all three partners in this dramatic event are equally to blame: the serpent for his cunning; the woman for her flatteries; and man for his weakness of character (72.7; II:230,15–16). Eve is not penalized more than the others. In fact, she is the symbol not so much of womankind as of humankind in general: 'O woman! The sweetness, delight, and beauty of the forbidden fruit is not yours. Or, if it be yours, by reason of the clod of earth from which man was formed, it is not yours alone: it is common to all living beings. What is specifically yours comes from elsewhere, and it is different: yours is all that in you is eternal and comes from eternity' (82.4; II:294,26–29). Surely it is possible to discern here the origin of what would later become the theme of the'eternal feminine'. Indeed, woman is the symbol of the highest realities: freedom, which God bestowed on her and on every other human being (82,4; II:295,1–7); wisdom (85.8; II;313,1–6); the soul, and the Church (61.2; II:149,14–15).

# CHAPTER II

# LETTERS
# TO WOMEN

*1. Women and Church reform.*

B ERNARD'S LETTERS to women do more than simply tell us something about those with whom he dealt or whom he occasionally mentioned in other works. They show us very explicitly the idea he had of women and the role they should play in the Church and in society.

We have twenty-three such letters. This is a good proportion if we compare Bernard with other letter-writers of his day. There are no letters to women in the collections of Peter of Celle and Stephen of Tournai. In the letter collection of Geoffrey of Vendôme, there are only two to women, and three in the collection of both Peter of Blois and Gilbert Foliot. Adam of Perseigne seems to have written ten letters to women, Yves of Chartres twelve, and Hildebert of Lavardin eighteen. Among John of Salisbury's three hundred twenty-five letters we find not a single one addressed to a woman, and he scarcely ever mentions women. Bernard tops the list, and to be complete, we should take into account the four letters written to married couples.

In about 1145 Bernard asked Geoffrey of Auxerre to compile an official collection of three hundred ten of his letters, a collection which he carefully and personally revised with a view to publication.[1] The idea of this *corpus* or, as it is often called, this register, was not conceived of as a source of information about people and events, but as a doctrinal work showing how the mystery of the Church should be lived out by its members. The order adopted is both chronological and ecclesiological. For each successive pontificate we find letters addressed to representatives of the different degrees within the Church structure, from the pope down through the hierarchy—archbishops, bishops, abbots—, and the whole non-clerical scale of political power—princes and nobles of various ranks, high and mighty ladies, abbesses, and nuns. It was Bernard's intention to compose, for each category in particular and for all of them as a whole, a sort of *speculum ecclesiae*, a mirror of the Church as he saw it, using historical events and symbolic persons. The Church could only be reformed—i.e. reformed to the teaching and example of Christ—if each member is himself reformed. Bernard's letters to the ladies of his day bear witness, then, as do all his other letters, to his christian anthropology and his ecclesiology. This does not mean that in telling these women how he would like them to be and what part they should play in the Church, Bernard never expressed the sentiments he felt for any of them.

This rather complex situation in which we find institutional, chronological and personal elements all tangled together, has made it no easy task to decide in which order to group these various texts. In the end it seemed best to classify them in accord with the social and ecclesiastical categories with which they deal and, within each category, by their object and temporal sequence.

---

[1] On this collection of Saint Bernard's letters and its nature as well as on the other letters of Bernard, see 'Recherches sur la collection des épîtres de saint Bernard', in *Cahiers de civilisation médiévale* 14 (1971) 205–219; 'Lettres de saint Bernard: histoire ou littérature?' in *Studi medievali* 12 (1971) 1–74.

This abundant and varied correspondence will only reveal its full meaning and content if we set it against the
historical background of the condition of women in the first
half of the twelfth century. We have to take into account a
new and growing awareness among both laymen and lay-
women of their own responsibility; the growing influence
of women in the political, religious, and literary fields; the
influence of the nobility; the increasing number of young
people, both boys and girls, who became interested in
knightly and courtly life; and lastly, in the area of marriage
laws, the stress laid on the equality of the two partners and
on their right to choose one another freely. These factors all
resulted from the gregorian reform, from demographic,
economic, and cultural developments, and from increased
relations with the East. They created new situations in
which Bernard found an opportunity for coming into contact with men and women in power, and even sometimes
men and women at the pinnacle of power. He wrote
more frequently to women in the world than to abbesses
and nuns, but he had a message for them, too. Writing
to all and sundry alike, he rarely did business without
adding a bit of advice or including some emotional out-
pouring. Bernard was a theologian and a reformer, but that
did not make him less a man, and as we shall see, a noble-
hearted man.

## 2. *Business and Counselling letters.*

As we have already seen, in the earliest of his extant
letters Bernard told his prior that a certain lady Beatrice had
intervened on his behalf.[2] He was at the time still a young
abbot and she was elderly, probably a widow, living qui-
etly near Clairvaux surrounded by her children and her
grandchildren. She took an interest in everything Bernard
did, and everything that concerned him: his health, his
goings about, his foundations; and she asked him to give

---

[2]See above, Chapter I, paragraph 3.

her news about it all.[3] In 1118 or 1119, Bernard did in fact write her an affectionate letter a whole page long (Ep 118; VII:298–299). In it he says: 'I admire the zeal of your devotion, the affection of your love. . . .' In Latin, this beautifully rhythmed sentence paves the way for an out-burst of grateful enthusing: the words delight (*dilectio*) and love (*amor*) recur several times. Bernard expresses surprise that she should show him such kindness when she is not his mother but his lady. She was not only an elderly benefactress, but also someone who comforted him in his time of sickness and convalescence which obliged him to live apart from his community. Rarely does Bernard give details in his letters about his health and his activities in the way he does here. Is he really confiding in the lady, or is he simply giving way to a bit of rhetorical exaggeration? Surely his monks and his family would have taken the trouble to enquire about him? Whatever the case, this is what he wrote: 'Who among my relatives and friends looks after me as well as you do? Who worries about my health the way you do? Does anyone among those I left behind in the world care so much for me, or even keep such memo-ries of me? Alas! Friends, relatives, neighbors, all consider me as someone long dead: you are the only one who cannot forget me.' He goes on to give details of his bouts of fever. He gives no advice and asks no favors. He is, quite simply, nice and affectionate.

Next in the register of his letters come two short mis-sives: one addressed to Simon, Duke of Lorraine, and to his wife, the Duchess Adelaide; the second to the duchess alone. We do not know the date when these letters were written, except that it was before 1139 (Epp 119–120; VII:299–301). In the first of them Bernard thanks the duke and the duchess for the 'friendliness and graciousness' they have shown both to himself and to the monks he had

---

[3]Damien van den Eynde in *Recueil d'études sur saint Bernard* III (Rome, 1969) 360.

sent out to make a foundation in their territory. He recommends that they show charity to all people, especially to those in greatest need. The tone of the letter, though not affectionate, is courteous. In the second letter, the one sent to the duchess alone, Bernard once more appeals to her good will that she may continue to be generous to the community of monks, and find a peaceful solution to some conflict which was going on. He says that he will comply with her lawful demands. Then he goes on to add: 'Through your lips, we greet the duke, and to him, as to yourself, we give this warning.' It was then an accepted thing that one of the roles of a christian wife was to make her husband gentle and this she was to do even as they were exchanging those 'chaste and dear embracings in which they took delight, so that in both of them the love of Christ might prevail.' This was the wish Bernard expressed in sending his letter, and he says not a single word about a rumor, reported by William of Saint Thierry, which had it that 'Adelaide's life was not so noble as her birth.'[4] Whatever the truth may be about that, she later, somewhere between 1139 and 1142, became a nun at Tart and her entry was the occasion of a decisive gesture of generosity toward the community.[5] If there was anything unfavorable to be said about Adelaide at some time in her life, Bernard is not the one who tells us about it. He does not even hint at such a thing.

The next letter in the register (Ep 121; VII:301–302) is earlier, written about the year 1120. In it Bernard asks a favor of Mathilda, duchess of Burgundy. We may wonder why he did not write to her husband, Hugh. Did he feel he had more chance of getting a hearing from a woman? He knew that she extended her friendship to him, and to the extent that, as he says, 'Anyone who feels that he has offended your dignity is fully confident that there is no easier way to get back into your favor than to go through

---

[4] William of Saint Thierry, *Vita prima Bernardi* I.68; *PL* 185:264.
[5] *Bernard de Clairvaux* (Paris, 1953) 419–420.

me.' That says a lot. Bernard immediately took advantage
of this situation to attempt to appease the displeasure one
of her subjects had raised in Mathilda, by persuading her to
let the man's son be allowed to marry the girl he wanted.
'Do this', wrote Bernard, 'out of love for God and for me.'
In the next part of the letter, the tone, though still calm,
became firmer. Bernard went so far as energetically to give
notice about some subject, leaving the final decision, however, with the duke. How nice that Bernard once again
approached the matter through the mediation of 'a very
dear noble lady' and that he intervened in favor of a man
of low estate and obtained his freedom to marry as he
pleased.

Among his letters which are not in the register, there are
several others addressed to women. Not only do they
confirm the impressions we get from the letters we have so
far examined, but they leave us asking the same questions.
There is no need to dwell on these letters here, but we may
take a look at two letters written at about the same period,
1149, to Sancia, sister of King Alphonsus of Castile and
Leon, and dealing with the same subject (Ep 301; VIII:
217–218). In the second letter she is called the king's 'maternal aunt.' Whatever her real relationship to the king, we
may wonder why it was specifically to her, and not to him,
that Bernard wrote asking for help and protection for a
monastery, especially as it meant intervening with several
bishops in order to find a solution to the conflict going on.
There is no doubt that Bernard had faith in the power
of women. Having won their affection, he made good use
of it.

Once when Mathilda, queen of England, wife of Henry I
Beauclerc, was staying at Boulogne, she showed great
affection for Bernard. In a letter written around 1142 (Ep
315; VIII:248), he reminded her of this to get her to keep a
promise she had once made to him concerning the monastery of La Capelle. About to give birth at the time,
she suddenly became so ill that, according to Geoffrey of

Auxerre, they began preparing for her funeral.[6] It occurred to her to invoke Bernard, and straightaway she gave birth to her child without the slightest difficulty. She immediately dispatched a messenger to Bernard to thank him, saying that the new-born child owed his life to him. Geoffrey adds that when Bernard was reminded of this he declined all responsibility and said jokingly : 'Am I really to be credited with that? Then it is certainly giving credit to someone totally unaware of it.' Yet now, to get the Queen to help him, he found a suitable moment to remind her of the event. He did it charmingly in the last sentence of his letter: 'Take great care of the son to whom you have just given birth. If I may say so without offence to the king, I am his father in a way, too.' Once more we are faced with the question of why he wrote to her, and not to him, in order to get some business peacefully arranged.

Bernard wrote to Mathilda again in 1142–1143, when he was hard at work advancing the cause of a cistercian monk to take the place of the benedictine William Fitzherbert who had been elected bishop of York. This time Bernard strongly advised the queen to take action with the king: 'If you could persuade my Lord King to oppose this sacrilege, in the presence of his bishops and princes, so that the right man and no other be appointed, any other solution being refused, it would give great honor to God, a guarantee of safety and security for the king, and the highest good of the whole kingdom.' (Ep 534; VIII:499). During this same controversy, Bernard even went so far as to write to a noblewoman, probably an influential matron at the roman court, so that the matter would be settled in the way he wanted (Ep 530; VIII:495). Though this note is a recommendation of certain abbots, it is really part of the Fitzherbert file, for in this affair Bernard used every means he had at his disposal.

---

[6]*Vita prima Bernardi* IV.6; *PL* 185:324–325. On the turbulent biography of Mathilda, see Regine Pernoud, *La femme au temps des cathédrales* (Paris, 1980) 153–158.

Finally, there is a short note of recommendation written at some uncertain date and sent to Adelaide, queen of France, wife of Louis VI (Ep 511; VIII:470). After a flattering phrase about the 'knowledge, friendship, generosity and kindness' she had shown him, Bernard gives her some specific and urgent advice on her duty to defend one of her subjects who had been unjustly condemned to exile. *Homo vester*, 'your man', he says, depends on you. But, we may ask, was he more dependent on the queen than on the king? He would seem to be the vassal of both king and queen, but primarily of the king. Why did Bernard appeal to womanly rather than manly qualities?

## 3. *Three Portraits*

Now let us take a look at what we might call the Melisande file. It contains four papers. This woman was the wife of count Fulk of Anjou who, in 1131, had become Fulk I, king of Jerusalem. He died in 1143 as a result of a fall from his horse. His widow acted as regent for more than ten years until their son was crowned as Baldwin III on 30 March 1152.[7] A first, undated, letter (Ep 206; VIII:65), which Bernard included in his official register, is a recommendation for one of his young cousins. Here again, as in the letter to Adelaide, Bernard began by reminding her that she had been very 'gracious' to him: 'Everyone knows that.' Are these just commonplaces, rhetorical formulas? The fact gave Bernard the right, not only to ask for help, but also to utter a warning: 'For the rest, take care that pleasures of the flesh and temporal glory do not hinder you on the way to the eternal kingdom.' Bernard's uncle Andrew, who was in Jerusalem, spoke favorably of Melisande. Here again, as in another earlier letter, he advised a great lady to take special care of the needy: pilgrims, paupers, and especially—a touching little detail—prisoners. He closes by asking her to keep him informed about

---

[7]Cf. *Bernard de Clairvaux*, 655.

everything concerning her person. We notice in this note his knack of gliding from niceness to frankness and firmness. It is almost as though, from afar, he kept an eye on this very important person who, according to most historians, lacked the requisite political wisdom.[8]

Another letter was sent around 1142 or 1143 (Ep 355; VIII:299). Bernard set about matters in the same way as before: 'See how much I trust you: I even dare to ask favors for other people'. In fact he was putting in a plea for the religious of the Premonstratensian Order, whom he presents as 'pacific combatants', called to take part in the 'Pilgrimage to the Holy Land'. Was Fulk I already dead? There is nothing to tell us for certain, but we notice that it was again to a queen that Bernard wrote, asking her to intervene.

This was followed shortly after by another, longer letter. This time we are sure that Melisande's husband was dead and that she had come to power. It was therefore within her right, so to speak, to accept the portrait of a model queen Bernard sketched with a firm hand. He had nothing to ask this time but was simply giving advice—the word recurs three times—'as a friend', as someone who 'loves not what she has but what she is'. Is she tempted to discouragement by the task ahead of her? Bernard comforts her energetically, instills confidence in her, forestalls any objection she might be tempted to raise because she is a woman, and persuades her that she is capable of discharging her difficult duty. What he says at the outset about the false vanity of passing glory could apply just as well to a king. But what he goes on to say about esteem for

---

[8]*Ibid.*, 389–390, 411, 415. By their very studied literary nature, or because of their doctrinal and psychological contents, some of Bernard's letters to women will be analysed here in detail. In preparing these, I am greatly indebted to Jean Figuet for Epp 113, 116–117, 289, 366. To him I should like to express my deepest gratitude.

women demonstrates his position in the matter and deserves being quoted here:

> Your husband is dead, the little king still incapable of bearing the weight of kingly affairs and of fulfilling his royal functions. All eyes look to you and on you alone falls the whole burden of government. You must give proof of courage and show manly energy even though you are a woman, putting the spirit of prudence and fortitude into all you do. You must arrange all things with wisdom and moderation, so that all who see you at work may look upon you more as a king than a queen and not ask 'Where is the King of Jerusalem?' But, you will say, 'I am not up to that. These are weighty things beyond my strength and my experience. That is a man's work and I am only a woman, physically weak, fickle of heart, incapable of foresight, little accustomed to business affairs'. I know my daughter, I know the importance of all that. But I know too that, however strong the storm, God in heaven is worthy of praise. That is a great thing. Yes, indeed, the Lord is great, and great is his strength.

The portrait gallery of Bernard's register still lacked a picture of the christian widow. Ten years after this last letter, in 1153, Bernard sketched this portrait of Melisande (Ep 289; VIII:205–206). In the interim he seems to have kept up a correspondence with her, for he begins by saying: 'I am surprised not to have received a letter from you in so long, and not to have received the greetings I am used to receiving. It is almost as though I had forgotten your long-standing oft-expressed devotedness to me.' Then, immediately afterwards, having prepared the way, as it were, by kind words, he let her know that he has heard some not very flattering echoes about her majesty and hastened to add that he would like not to believe what he had heard. From his uncle, Andrew, he has also received a message to reassure him: according to the uncle, she protected the Knights Templar and governed with the wisdom God has

bestowed on her. Here again Bernard found an opportunity to praise the great things a woman can do in her
widowhood. This is a state of life which makes its own
demands, and a woman is all the more obliged to keep to
them when she willingly remains a widow. Bernard reminded Melisande that she was free to remarry after her
husband's death. If she chose not to do so, she must accept
the consequences.

What follows is very lofty in tone and couched in a very
refined literary style. Certainly Bernard took great pains to
carve out this program, intended for publication, for the
life-style of someone obliged to reconcile the duties of a
queen with those of a widow. His main source was Saint
Paul: the Bridegroom to be loved as the Lord himself.
Melisande was left to draw her own conclusions from this
friendly warning. Bernard asked her to renew her friendship with him and to recommence her habit of writing to
him often.

The originality of this very artistically written text lies in
Bernard's ability to speak not only of the duties incumbent
on a widow, but also very subtly to weave in the respon-
sibilities of a queen. Just as queenship brings out in a
woman certain qualities which a man does not have, so
widowhood provides the opportunity for putting into
practice other womanly qualities:

> All that, of course, suits a brave woman, a widow who
> has remained humble even though raised to the rank
> of queen. Indeed, it is not because you are a queen
> that widowhood lies beneath your dignity, for you
> would not be a widow had you not chosen to remain
> one. I think that your particular glory, especially in the
> eyes of Christians, derives from the fact that you
> manage to live equally as widow and queen. Queen-
> ship is the result of succession, widowhood of virtue.
> The one is yours by birth, the other is a gift of God.
> The one came to you by birth, the other you acquired
> by manly courage. You have two honors: one accord-

ing to the world, the other according to God; but both come from God. Do not consider the honor of widowhood as being of little account for the Apostle Paul has said: 'Honor widows who are real widows' (1 Tm 5:3).

Finally, we have the portrait of a mother worried about her young son (Ep 300; VIII:216–217). Bernard wrote to Mathilda, countess of Blois, around the year of 1152:

If you think your son has exceeded his limits with you, we are indeed sorry. And we deplore just as much the excesses of the son as the wrong done to his mother. Yet the young lad can plead some excuses. The youthful faults he has committed are to be excused by the tendencies natural to his age. Surely you know that the heart of man is bent downward and that in adolescence his thoughts turn to evil? You must trust and hope that the merits and alms of his father will effect a change. You must besiege God more and more with promises and prayers . . . Yes! let us pray and groan before the Lord that God may bring back to a sense of duty a young man of such happy disposition, able to imitate his father's honesty, as we have no doubt. But you must show him a spirit of gentleness and lavishly cajole him, for in this way he will be moved to do good far more than if he were to be embittered by vexing words and reproaches. If we adopt this method we shall soon both rejoice at the change in him. You know full well that I am as anxious as you to see him come back to a better frame of mind. If only he behaved with you as he has always done with me, for I do not think that he has ever refused to comply with my least wish.

Having reminded both father and mother of their responsibility towards their son, Bernard betrays his closer feeling for the mother, and he hopes that she will imitate him.

## 4. *To Ermengard: Intimate Letters.*

Two letters to Ermengard (Ep 116–117; VII:296–297), though not long, have surprised, even disconcerted, more than one of Bernard's readers. They contain affective, in fact tender, outpourings which one hardly expects from his pen. They are well worth looking at from the point of view, not only of history and literary style, but also psychology and spirituality. They were written at some uncertain date not later than 1135, when Bernard was at most forty-five years old.

Who was this Ermengard? According to Bernard's two letters, she had once been a high and mighty countess, but was now a widow. She had also lost her son and lives now without social position, without noble rank, and without wealth. As we shall see, Bernard had a lot to say about the spiritual frame of mind he attributed to her. But what do we know about her from other sources? Was she one of Bernard's converts and even 'quite a strange convert', as some have conjectured?[9] In the foundation charter of the Abbey of Buzay, in 1135, her son, the duke of Brittany, Conan III, stated that 'she took the veil recently and was consecrated by the hands of the abbot of Clairvaux at the priory of Larrey', near Dijon.[10] Some historians think that this event took place in 1130, or at least between 1129 and 1135. But later her son asked her to join him in the Holy Land. Various opinions on this were passed by Geoffrey of Vendôme, a contemporary chronicler, and others after him, and it all remains shrouded in some mystery. Bernard does not help us see things more clearly. All we can gather from his letters is that she was still in France, close enough to Clairvaux for Bernard to consider dropping in to see her from time to time. She lived detached from family ties and the fortune she had once had. The fact that Bernard says

---

[9]*Bernard de Clairvaux*, 421.

[10]The most recent biographical notice on Ermengard is that by Regine Pernoud, *La femme au temps des cathédrales* (Paris, 1980) 143–149.

nothing in his letters about the circumstances of her life confirms the thesis that, in his correspondence as a whole, he aimed not at giving historians chronological information but simply at passing along a spiritual message to all.[11]

This being so, what was the message and how did Bernard want to pass it on? In a very literary way, certainly. Some notable corrections were made to the letter 117 as given in the short and the long collections and, in the long collection, to letter 116. Even so, both letters in their first draft are full of nice touches which we should point out in analyzing the text.

The missive's beginning and its conclusion set the tone: 'To his dear one... loving affection'. The words affection, delight, charity occur four times in nineteen lines, together with words like 'heart' and 'marrow', which conjure up the notion of intimacy. Every word, every turn of phrase, is so full of subtle echoes that no translation can ever catch them. Before commenting them, however, let us give a summary of each. First, letter 116:

> Would to God that you could read my heart as you do this parchment. You would then see what deep love the finger of God has engraved there, and very quickly you would see that neither tongue nor pen are able to express what the Spirit of God has put into the very depths of my being. My heart is close to you even though I am absent in body. If you cannot perceive this, you have only to descend into your own heart and there you will find mine. You cannot doubt that I feel for you as much affection as you feel for me, unless you think that you love me more than I do you, and that you have a higher opinion of your own heart than of mine in matters of affection.

---

[11]This was the conclusion of the study: 'Lettres de saint Bernard: histoire ou littérature?' in *Studi medievali* 12 (1971) 1–74.

And now the gist of the second note:

My heart is filled with joy when I hear that yours is at peace. Your joy is my joy and your cheerful radiance brings health to my soul. How I would have enjoyed talking with you about all this instead of writing it in a letter. I must admit that I do sometimes feel a grudge against all the businesses which prevent my coming to see you. I am so happy when they allow me to do so. This does not happen often, it is true; but rare as it may be, I could not be happy at it, because I should rather see you only from time to time than not see you at all. I hope to visit you soon; and I am already looking forward to it.

From the start, the first text looks like one of those 'love jousts', examples of which abound in the love literature of the times: who loves whom more. Bernard did everything he could to show Ermengard how much he loved her. But he betrays a certain tentativeness; he cannot be sure of success. And certainly it was not easy to prove his love: 'Ah! if only I could...Ah! if only you could... No tongue can ever express what the Spirit of God has graven in the depths of my being!' This cannot be uttered because it belongs to an order higher than that of nature or the human mind.' Bernard uses negations (*nec...nec*) in his attempt to convey this and then he adds his wish, 'May I appear to you... May you guess...'. Then there is a change in tone: the imperative voice is used three times: 'Descend into your heart then... Look... Give me some love too...'. Who loves more? Having supposed that there is mutual love, Bernard goes on to mention the quantity of love, using words such as 'more', 'less', then 'how' it is present. 'It is for you to see about your love', he says. As for himself, he has a final word which is a flash of inspiration worthy of Bernard as both lover and author for, in one concise formula, we have a play on both words and meaning: *Nusquam abs te absque te recedo....* Not very much later, Marie de France in her *Honeysuckle Lay (Lai du*

*Chèvrefeuille*) puts into Tristan's mouth the words the honeysuckle spoke to the service tree it was entwining: 'Neither you without me, nor me without you.'[12]

The last sentence of this note is realistic. Bernard is 'on
the way' (*in via*) and even in transit (*in transitu*), which
explains the brevity of the message. But he holds out hope
of a longer letter later, if he has time and God allows. This
attitude, compared with that of another monk writing and
moaning at length to a lady recluse friend, far away,[13]
shows that Bernard was a man of action: he had no time to
waste; he knew he was in God's hands.

So far we have seen Bernard's lack of doubt about his
feelings for Ermengard, and about hers for him. But did he
wonder whether she realized how much he loved her?
How could he express what he knew to have been impressed in his heart by God himself? The latin verbs Bernard
uses, *imprimere* and *exprimere*, impress and express, were
heralded by the word he used to indicate that he wanted to
open up, to expand (*expandere*), his soul to Ermengard. In
all this there are obviously formulas from Exodus 24:12,
which mentions the law graven by the very finger of God,
and from Saint Paul's epistle to the Galatians (4:6) where
he speaks of the Spirit of God at work 'in our hearts' where
'he even writes a letter' (2 Cor 3:2–3). It was up to Bernard
to express by tongue and pen what God had impressed on
him. The difficulty of expressing what only 'experience
teaches' (SC I.11; I:7,28–30) is a specifically bernardine
theme. It has to do with the transition from interiority—
suggested by the prefix *in-* to the outward spoken or written word suggested by *ex*. In the case of Bernard and

---

[12]'Bele amie, si est de mis: Ne vus sanz mei, ne jeo sanz vus', quoted
and commented by P. Menard, *Les lais de Marie de France* (Paris, 1979)
137–138.

[13]This text has been edited by C.H. Talbot, 'The Liber confortatorius of
Goscelin of Saint Bertin', in *Analecta monastica. Textes et études sur la vie
des moines au Moyen Age* III, Studia monastica 37 (Rome, 1955) 1–117. This
will be the subject of a special study.

Ermengard, it was a matter of her really believing in his affection.

Once this had been assured, everything essential was done, and physical presence mattered little. Bernard used Saint Paul's own words in assuring the Corinthians: 'though absent in body, I am present in spirit' (1 Cor 5:3). Bernard came back to this later with the irony, or rather humor, characteristic of detachment, saying that it would be better for them to see one another from time to time than not at all, and the very thought of such joy is already a foretaste of it.

The Creator has 'touched' (*affecit*) Ermengard and Bernard, who says that their role in this God inspired love is a passive one. Bernard, thus touched, moved—or, better still, pushed—by God, reacts by calling to her attention all that God has done. Both this letter and the following show how Bernard strove to reveal this truth, and this accounts for words like 'Truth to say', 'I confess', 'believe me'. He invited Ermengard to a similar acknowledgement of what was going on inside her: 'near you', 'descend into your heart', 'what you feel to be present there', 'to experience'. This is all part of a reflection on love. Such language can, of course, be interpreted purely as a psychological phenomenon. But why not credit it also with some faith value since Bernard thought it had one, and said so, at least as far as he was concerned?

And what was his correspondent's experience? The love joust admits the possibility of a difference between the partners, but it tends to balance things by equally strong feelings on both sides. Rivalry may pose some danger to humility. Bernard insinuates this discreetly: 'If you presume to rise above me because you love me more, let it be to the degree that you consider me overwhelmed by your charity.' This interplay between charity and humility comes up again in the following letter, where it is expressed in an interplay of prefixes and assonances, like *humilis ex sublimi* and other paradoxes suggestive of lowliness coming from grandeur, humility from sublimity. This is all strewn with biblical reminiscences, subtle, but sufficiently clear to bring to mind the humility of the Virgin Mother—'what has been born in you of the Holy Spirit' (cf Lk 1:35)—'the love which Saint John says casts out fear (1 Jn 4:18), the conception within ourselves of what Isaiah calls the Spirit of Salvation, (26:18), the radical refusal to attribute to self anything which does not come truly from God: 'neither to me nor to you', reminds us of Jesus refusing Mary's request at Cana during the wedding feast (Jn 2:4) as well as his refusal to Peter, and even to Satan (Mk 5:7). So Bernard could come round to saying outright to Ermengard: 'The rest depends on your modesty. . . .'.

The tone of letter 117 is very different, even though the style is the same. The dominant theme is 'joy', the mutual joy they take in one another. This joy could be marred—'I am vexed'—by Bernard's inability to meet Ermengard because of his own occupations. Yet here again, Bernard was a realist and even an optimist: not only is a bit better than nothing, but this 'bit' becomes still more precious. There is a cascade of word plays: occupations-opportunities; *cara-rara; impediri-expediri*. These last two couplets defy translation. Between desire and reality there is total opposition: occupations are frequent, opportunities are rare: 'if only from time to time'. And this gives rise to contrary sentiments: 'I am vexed', 'I am delighted'— *irascor-delector*. But the tone of the letter is still light and pleasant, in no way dramatic: occupations are endured, opportunities seized. And the result is the cherished, if rare, friendly meeting. The conclusion alludes to the ending of the two epistles in which Saint John regrets not seeing his dear ones again but mixes with it the perspective of a perfect and lasting joy (2 Jn 11:12; 3 Jn 13–14). Bernard speaks of a 'coming and complete joy', echoing the merriment expressed at the beginning of the letter. Between them he twice uses the word 'alacrity', in the sense of exhilaration and liveliness.

In these two short texts we see Bernard animated by a desire, never cloying yet never upsetting, that he be known to love. He gives proof of ardor and balance, of good spiritual health and vigor. Why, we may ask, did he want these two notes to be included in his register? Surely they are more of a private nature? There is no doubt that these texts with their studied, even precious, style must have given great pleasure to the former countess of Brittany. They could not fail to bring her honor. But there is in them much more than the amusement of a man of letters: they contain a teaching which Bernard leaves attentive readers to discover. This language of love resembles the language of 'separated love' found in all love literature, the 'love from afar', *'amor delongh '* that we read about in twelfth-century romances. The reality on which it is founded is the dialectic of absence and presence by which real presence, the one most real because it is spiritual, is available only at the price of physical absence. Now all that can be said of human love between two persons can be applied to the religious plane, and, in fact, it is only perfectly accomplished at that level.[14] What is more, in this context, the word and the image 'heart', the place and also the witness of this presence, takes on a new meaning: the interiority which requires lucid discernment and detachment.

At the same time these two letters tell us about the affection between two human beings with hearts capable of love, they pre-suppose—and teach—a spiritual formation of love. Affection is to be acknowledged and not repressed; it is to be purified, lifted up, transformed, into a condition of renunciation. Our love relationship with God requires that we commit our whole being to him and that we consent to a sacrifice joyfully accepted in faith. When affection exists between two persons, each gives and

---

[14]Father G. de Broglie has shown how the language of courtly love in the twelfth century could be, and was, applied in expressions of devotion to the sacred heart: 'Le "coeur" à partir du XIIe siècle', in *Fête du Sacré-Coeur*, Assemblées du Seigneur, 56 (Paris) 84–87.

receives to the fullest, going beyond self and helping the other to do the same. When Bernard revealed his heart to Ermengard, telling her in courtly, almost playful, terms what her own heart should be, he gives us a glimpse—but without stressing the point as he does elsewhere[15]—of the possibility of an unbounded love not only between humans, but also between human beings and God. This limitless love goes by the christian name 'charity'.

---

[15]For example, in the case of William of Saint Thierry and Oger the canon. See 'Saint Bernard psychothérapeute' in *Nouveau visage de saint Bernard*, 27–30 [*A Second Look at St Bernard* (Kalamazoo, 1989)].

# CHAPTER III

# BERNARD
# AND NUNS

## 1. *The Charmer.*

B ERNARD DID NOT WRITE much to nuns. It was not that
he was not interested in them. He was, very actively, and chiefly because he was the originator of
many a nun's vocation. At the age of twenty he literally
'preached' on behalf of the monastic life to his fellows, his
friends, and members of his family, and persuaded many
of the menfolk to go with him to Cîteaux. Is it possible that
the girls were unmoved by this? William of Saint Thierry
tells us that he was a charmer and that people took precautions against him: 'As he was preaching, either in public or
in private, mothers hid their sons, wives kept their husbands near themselves, and friends kept their friends away
from him, for the Holy Spirit gave such persuasion to his
words that a man's bonds to any other person could hardly
bear the strain.'[1] We do not find this statement in the
*Fragmenta* where Geoffrey of Auxerre tells about this period of Bernard's life, so we may wonder whether it is not
just William's interpretation, or perhaps exaggeration.
What are the facts?

That Bernard converted countless young men and adults
to the monastic life then and later, is well known. His field

---

[1]*Vita prima Bernardi* I.15; *PL* 185:235.

of action was the feudal aristocracy of his own region. But equally, and throughout the rest of his life, he had some influence on women. With some of them he was very demanding, as we have seen in his letters to noblewomen. He had a knack for asking and getting two things. The first was generosity to monasteries in which he had a particular interest, especially Cîteaux itself, for a monastic foundation requires more than fervent intentions; it needs lands and buildings, and therefore donations. At the very time of Bernard's own conversion, a woman saved Cîteaux from destitution. She was the lady of the manor of Verzy, Elizabeth, the daughter of Count Savory of Donzy. She had great possessions in Burgundy and enlarged the holdings of Cîteaux enough to enable the abbey to continue to exist. Without her, the band of friends Bernard brought with him to Cîteaux could never have been taken in. Her generous gifts continued during the decisive period between the close of 1109 and 1112. But the countess could not make these decisions alone. Though she is the first mentioned in the charter, she could do nothing without the consent of her husband and her sons. Yet, it was from her and through her that Cîteaux and Bernard obtained these donations. Her husband and his heirs confirmed her contracts, renouncing their claim to the lands handed over to the monks.[2]

Such largess could scarcely pass without comment in the neighboring countryside. Nor could Bernard's entry at Cîteaux in April 1112 with thirty-two companions, all of whom were close relatives or friends, some bachelors like himself, some married men. What was Bernard to do for his sisters-in-law, his cousins, and the wives of his married

---

[2]Jean de la Croix Bouton, *Histoire de l'ordre de Cîteaux* (Westmalle, 1959) 75–76. Instances of the conversion of noble families underlying monastic foundations have been illustrated by J. Wolhasch, 'Parenté noble et monachisme réformateur. Observations sur les ''conversions'' à la vie monastique' in *Revue historique* 264 (1980) 3–24.

friends? Here we see another place where Bernard exerted his charm and made claims on women. We should not overlook the fact that his arrival at Cîteaux coincided with a rush of vocations to women's monasteries. All these vocations came from the same feudal milieu as did the men Bernard brought to the monastery. Is this coincidence merely chance, or did the first have something to do with the second? In the face of facts like this the words of William of Saint Thierry take on their full meaning.

Sometime around 1113, Count Miles of Bar founded the monastery of Jully for nuns on one of his lands. It happens that Bernard's uncle Rainald, a relative of Bernard's mother, Aleth, was one of the count's vassals. It is not unlikely that he intervened with his lord in this matter. The first prioress was Elizabeth, the wife of Bernard's eldest brother Guy. Around 1128 she was succeeded in office by Humbeline, Bernard's sister.[3] And it was Bernard, along with other abbots, who drew up the statutes of the community which stipulated that the number of nuns should never exceed seventy. These precautionary measures were designed to forestall excessive prosperity, signs of which had already set in. The same statutes also stated that no one under the age of fifteen was to be admitted—one more indication that Cistercians were refusing to admit to their monasteries, children, boys or girls, offered by their families as oblates.[4] The rush to monasteries consisted of young adults. The monastery of Jully was not yet fully cistercian, but was already 'bernardine' because of the major role he and his family played in its foundation and development.

It was Jully that provided the abbess of the first truly cistercian monastery for nuns, founded in 1125 at Tart and destined to become the head of a congregation numbering eighteen houses in all. Manual labor, even tilling the soil,

---

[3] J. de la Croix Bouton, *Histoire . . .*, 118.
[4] *Études sur saint Bernard et le texte de ses écrits* (Rome, 1954) 194.

was held in honor there. Enclosure seems to have been less strict than at Jully, for the nuns went out in groups to work outside the enclosure. Part of the abbess' charge was to give permission for these outings.[5]

Among women converts to monastic life under Bernard's influence, we notice first Adelaide, duchess of Lorraine, to whom Bernard wrote the letter we analyzed in the preceding chapter. When she became a nun around 1139 or 1140, her son agreed to make the foundation. She died in 1153, the same year as Bernard himself.[6] Others included Adeline and her mother, both members of Bernard's family. They became canonesses at Poulangy and from there transferred to a cistercian monastery affiliated to Tart whose prioress was Bernard's niece, Adeline. In 1149–1150, the whole community of Poulangy turned cistercian.[7] Some cases of transfer among monks caused a certain uproar, but transfers of nuns made less noise and fuss. Among both the men and the women, however, Bernard was behind the change.

Finally, we have an example of some nuns' admiration for Bernard which has long been ignored: the nuns of the Paraclete and their abbess Heloise.[8] As early as January 1131, Bernard and Abelard were both part of the entourage of Innocent II when he visited the Abbey of Morigny, near Étampes. The abbot of Clairvaux, ardently devoted to Innocent's cause during the Anacletan schism, surely put in a good word for the abbey founded by Heloise and Abelard. Only a few months later, it received the privilege of papal recognition. Shortly afterwards, it seems Bernard

---

[5]Bouton, *Histoire. . .* , 119–124.

[6]*Bernard de Clairvaux*, 419–420.

[7]*Ibid.*, 420–421.

[8]Chrysogonus Waddell, 'Saint Bernard and the Cistercian Office at the Abbey of the Paraclete', in E.R. Elder-J. Sommerfeldt, edd., *The Chimaera of His Age. Studies in Bernard of Clairvaux* (Kalamazoo: Cistercian Publications, 1980) 76.

paid a visit to the Paraclete which Abelard mentions in a letter to him:

> I went recently to the Paraclete to settle some business. Your daughter in Christ, and our sister, who is abbess there, tells me that to her great joy you paid them a holy visit which they had been waiting for for a long time. She says that it was more as an angel than as a man that you comforted both her and her sisters with holy exhortations. She confided to me in private that because of the special charity you have for me, you were a little upset that the Lord's prayer is not recited in the usual way at all the Hours in their chapel. . . .

And Abelard goes on to explain at length why he had the nuns adopt this custom.[9]

Did Bernard return several times to the Paraclete? Clairvaux is not far away and it is quite possible he did. A careful examination of the liturgy of the Paraclete shows that several hymns composed by Abelard especially for the nuns were replaced by texts from the cistercian liturgy reformed under Bernard's supervision. One historian has called this the 'deabelardization' of the Paraclete liturgy. Bernard too composed liturgical pieces in which he harmoniously combined traditional aesthetics with the exuberance proper to his age of troubadours and trouvéres.[10] Abelard's texts probably sounded too intellectual. And we must not forget that the Abbey of Tart was not far away. Bernard seems to have exerted a really irresistible influence.

## 2. *Project Letters.*

Everything Bernard wrote on monastic life for monks applied equally to nuns, but he made a special point of

---

[9] Abelard, Ep 10; *PL* 178: 335.
[10] C. Waddell, (n.53) 108–109.

leaving them some specific messages. There are only three, but they cover a whole set of problems. Since they are what we might call project-letters, general in nature, the recipients are to all intents and purposes anonymous, as for example his letter to young Sophia.

The first of the three was written to an unidentified nun, perhaps no one in particular but a symbol of a spiritual state which provided an opportunity for writing about her (Ep 114; VII:291–293).[11] It would have been easy to sketch the portrait of the model nun. But that existed already in many other texts. Bernard preferred to write about ongoing conversion: after a crisis which had become something of a second conversion, the nun had found new fervor. Bernard heard about it and the news filled him with joy, indeed 'perfect joy'. These and equivalent words abound in the first lines, where they are set in contrast with others expressing tears and sadness. Bernard's joy, and that of his correspondent, was interior: there was no outward success, no visible prosperity. As he says, this is something very personal: 'Examine yourself: you know yourself better than I do. Is this not what the Holy Spirit who dwells in your heart is crying out to you?' And then comes praise for womanhood, in words Bernard loved: although this nun is young, beautiful, and of noble birth— all qualities savoring of worldliness—, although she is weak by reason of her sex, she rises above such frailty, renounces any advantages she may so far have enjoyed, and now 'breathes happy freedom'. Bernard went on to contrast the values pleasing to God and the world, interior values and exterior. Far from all transitory values the nun now 'begins to live again'. She lives no longer for the world, but for Christ and in Christ, by dying with him and for him.

---

[11]According to a manuscript cited in the critical apparatus, p. 291, the recipient would seem to have been a member of the Abbey of Sainte-Marie at Troyes; but this variant in a single witness is probably explained by the fact that the next letter is addressed to a nun of this monastery.

Only after all this does Bernard go on to a few words of praise for virginity. In this, as in all else, what matters is truth: a person's life-style must be in keeping with the state professed and the habit worn. He writes: 'Do they not call you a nun and a monastic?' The first of the latin words he uses, *nonna et sanctimonialis*, was rare at that time. Then he plays on words, like *velatum elatum*, veiled, uplifted; *wimplatae magis quam velatae*, which might be clumsily translated 'wimpled rather than veiled'. The allusion to a wimple (or gimp) summons up images of how women in the world dressed. He also has *vitam-vestem*, life and garb. But he soon comes back to the essential: the Holy Spirit's presence within her, the ardent Spirit who fills her heart inwardly with the flame whose fire urges her to meditation. The conclusion is one long play on ten words, and images of kindling a fire and extinguishing it. There is no doubt that Bernard was having a bit of literary fun: he gave pleasure to nuns not only by excusing any possible moments of mediocrity, and by encouraging them to press forward but also by making them smile by his flashes of literary wit.

This first manifesto for fervor found its way into the register, as did the letter to Sophia. We find another there as well, (Ep 115; VII:294–295). It throws light on a matter which has generally been studied mainly in connection with monks, but also concerned women, both lay and religious: the attraction of the solitary life. The first half of the twelfth century was marked in the Church by a strong eremitical trend which caused the appearance of hermits of every sort, with varied forms of life and activity, some of them weird and even dangerous. Saint Bernard and the Cistercians thought they had found a remedy to all this by creating a kind of cenobitic eremitism, a solitary life in community. But among Cistercians, as among every other religious institution the very prosperity of the Order and increasing membership soon revived a desire for more real personal solitude. Bernard found himself frequently obliged to write to monks warning them against this call to solitude which he considered an illusion and a temptation.[12] Nuns did not escape it.

One of them was a member of Saint Mary's Abbey, Troyes, a town not far from Clairvaux. At some unknown date Bernard wrote that he had heard talk about her. 'Her spiritual mother and her sisters are trying to dissuade her' from pursuing her intention. So she turned to Bernard for advice. His solution was radical, even though he started out by professing prudence: 'I think and think again, I dare not judge hastily. . .'. Yet after this careful preparation, he lays his cards on the table: 'Absolutely not, *Nequaquam*. . .'. He then went on to compare the dangers and the advantages of both the solitary and the cenobitic life, all to the advantage of the second, of course. In order to 'take away any excuse for error', he drew this parallel from the Gospel: 'You are either one of the foolish virgins—supposing you are a virgin—or one of the wise. In the first case you need the community; in the second the community needs you'. As Bernard saw things, the common good counts more than anything else. The abbey of Troyes had just gone through a spiritual renewal; to leave it now would only help to 'cover it with shame and weaken it', *infamabitur aut infirmabitur*. Here again we find one of those word plays which Bernard used to render a hard message more acceptable by couching it in a pleasing style. He confidently detected in the call to the solitary life the 'serpent's virus', and begs the nun to recognize it too. With his pen he sketched out terrifying images of a solitary life in the forest: shadows, wolves, the lambkin left to herself falling prey. 'Listen to me, my daughter, listen to my good advice. Whether saint or sinner, never wander far from the flock. There you are better set for avoiding sin and for

---

[12] 'L'érémitisme et les cisterciens' in *L'eremitismo in Occidente nei secoli XIᵉ XII* (Milan, 1965) 573–576. On the hermit life among Cistercians after Saint Bernard's time, see esp. 580.

doing good to your companions.' For Bernard the decisive element in this matter of conscience was not what the person herself felt, but what her abbess and her sisters thought would most contribute to the true good of everyone concerned. This message, marked by common sense and charity, as well as literary value, which does no harm, was certainly worth publishing in the register. It is of value to both monks and nuns.

Finally there is the file—only part of which is in the register—on a special case: the abbey of the benedictine nuns of Favernay (Ep 391; VIII:360–361). The buildings needed repair and the abbess, Odoarde had set about having them made. Bernard congratulated her on this and took the opportunity to warn her to be careful about the good management of her community and of a hospice which depended on it, and of a priest who lived there. He gave some practical advice as to how she should go about things and recommended she go on trusting him as one of the family. But Bernard's advice had no effect, and in 1132, the benedictine monks of Chaise-Dieu took over Favernay and sent one of their own monks over. He turned out to be an embezzler who persecuted, among others, the cistercian abbot Guy of Cherlieu.[13] In 1141 Bernard defended Guy and strongly rebuked Peter of Traves, dean of Besançon (Ep 197; VIII:53); he also sent a hot letter to Innocent II (Ep 198; VIII:54), denouncing the culprit again as well as his protector, the abbot of Chaise-Dieu (Ep 199; VIII:56–57). Whether or not Bernard's warnings had any effect, we do not know; nor do we know the outcome of the whole affair. What is certain is that Bernard stood up powerfully against a church dignitary, a powerful abbot, and one of his monks in order to safeguard the interest of a community of nuns.

---

[13]*Bernard de Clairvaux*, 225; and Mgr Pirolley, *L'hostie sauvée des flammes* (Paris, 1950) 25–26.

## 3. Hildegard of Bingen

Hildegard was the abbess of a traditional monastery—
thus not cistercian—at Bingen on the Rhine, from about
1148 onward.[14] She had visions and claimed to 'see' certain
people, sometimes highly placed persons, and all that
should be praised or censured in them. She decided to
write to tell them about this and did so with the help of
Wolmar of Rupertsberg, a monk from the neighboring
benedictine abbey. It was beginning to cause problems for
Hildegard and for others concerned. The question arose:
are these visions authentic? There was a great deal of talk
going on about them. It was true that she had vast knowledge of God and his mysteries and was also well versed in
the psychology of both men and women. She wrote on
extremely varied subjects. In 1141 she started the *Scivias*, a
general survey which she completed in 1151.

At the beginning of 1149, Bernard was travelling in the
Rhineland to promote the second crusade, but, although
he twice passed not far from Bingen,[15] he did not go out of
his way to visit the abbey. Sufficiently confident of his
mission, since it had been mandated by Eugene III, he saw
no reason for consulting a visionary and did not have the
curiosity to go and hear the oracles of a woman who was
already considered, and would one day be officially recognized as a prophetess. Bernard had firm convictions about
the scale of values and the hierarchy of the different mani-
festations of church life and that was enough to make him
prefer an order from the pope to any private revelation. It is

---

[14]On the biography of Saint Hildegard, see A. Führkötter, *Das Leben
der heiligen Hildegard von Bingen. Herausgegeben, eingeleitet und Übersetzt*
(Düsseldorf, 1968); on the chronology relative to the period dealt with
here, *ibid.*, 130–131; more recently: M-L. Arduini, '''Pauperes'' et ''pau-
pertas'' nella Renania dei secoli XIᵉ XII. Ruperto di Deutz, santa
Ildegarda di Bingen' in *Instituzioni monastiche e canoniche in Occidente
(1123–1215)* (Milan, 1980) 647–659.

[15]On Bernard's trip, see E. Russel, 'Bernard et les dames de son
temps' in *Bernard de Clairvaux* (Paris, 1953) 423.

probably because not everyone understood and recognized the assurance of both Bernard and the abbess that it was later found necessary to invent a legendary visit the abbot made to Hildegard, in the course of which they were reputed to have exchanged presents.[16]

About this same time, at some undetermined date around 1146–1147, Hildegard decided to write to Bernard.[17] She told of her admiration for him and said that some years earlier she had had a vision in which she saw him in such dazzling light that it brought tears to her eyes and left her full of confusion, 'blushing and timid'. After this profession of humility she went on to ask his advice in complete trust: 'See how I rise and run to you.'. What she says next proves that she had an accurate understanding of one aspect of Bernard's unique charism, travelling for the good of the Church: 'You move about, but you sustain others. You are the eagle fixing your eyes on the sun. Put these words in your heart and never cease to fix your eyes on God for me.'

By its restraint Bernard's reply (Ep 366; VIII:323–326) contrasts with Hildegard's outpourings of praise. The text is brief: no more than twelve lines in all. It is so short, in fact, that the next generation thought it necessary to add a few lines which contribute nothing new in the way of ideas, but stress the encouragements already given.[18]

In the authentic text, how did Bernard react to the flattery in this letter from this churchwoman, an acknowledged mystic? His style, though restrained, is not curt. He starts off, in fact, by affirming his affection: 'To his beloved daughter in Christ, Hildegard. . .' The word used is *dilectae*: beloved. Beloved of whom? God? Or Bernard? Both, as

---

[16] Russel, 423, note 67.

[17] *PL* 197: 189–190.

[18] In SBOp VIII: 323–324, the long text is provided in the apparatus giving variants. On these two drafts of the letter see 'Nouveaux témoins de la survie de saint Bernard 3. La diffusion de la lettre à Hildegarde' in *Homenaje a Fray Justo Perez de Urbel, OSB* (Silos, 1977) 104–106.

we see by what follows. Already in the first word there is at least some encouragement: she may rest assured that she is not held in suspicion, but loved. It is 'in Christ' that she is loved and as a 'daughter' to both God and Bernard. We see here an immediate and straight-forward answer, not only to Hildegard's own hesitations, but also to those of the churchmen who wondered about her visions. Bernard reassured both her and them. And he did so in the salutation, by saying he was writing as a 'brother', 'called' by God to be 'abbot of Clairvaux', but also as a 'sinner'; and as a sinner he was praying for her. This was a joust of humility between the two of them. At the same time there is a rigid literary structure in this short piece, because the final sentence which the longer text develops begins with a formula conveying the notion of intense prayer: *'Rogamus magis et suppliciter postulamus . . .* We beg, rather we insistently implore . . .'

Acts of humility and charity are inserted between these two attitudes of prayer. In the first sentence Bernard refuses to play at being an oracle: there is a mirror image between the humility Hildegard showed in her letter and Bernard's humility in his reply. 'It is, I think, your own humility, and that alone, which accounts for your having a very different opinion of my conscience than I do'. This last allusion begins the dominant theme, that each person should examine himself. Bernard made it his duty to reply, but only briefly because of his many occupations—a set phrase which we find elsewhere,[19] and to which we should attach no particular significance.

Immediately after this introduction come the decisive words: 'We are very happy about this grace God has given you'. In the Latin of this sentence there is a play on words stressing the gift, the charism received from God: *'Congratulemur gratiae . . .'*. The grace which is in you. We find this in Saint Paul's letter to Timothy (1 Tm 4:14;2 Tm 1:6). Then

---

[19] For example, at the end of the letter to Ermengarde, Ep 116; VII:296.

Bernard very explicitly affirms that Hildegard has received a gift from God: 'this grace is really in you'. And he adds that she must at all costs consider it a grace which has an immediate consequence: 'so you must respond to it with all possible humility and devotion', devotion meaning both devotedness to God and piety. This is supported by a statement from Scripture, the only one to be found in this letter, but a very important one. It is taken from the Letter of Saint James (4:6) and is preceded by a phrase reminding her that this depends on the knowledge which comes from faith: 'You know this full well: God opposes the proud but gives grace to the humble'. The word 'grace', used here for the third time in four lines, once more stresses the link between humility and God's gift.

'In what concerns me —*Quod in nobis est*—this then is what I exhort and beseech you to do'. Bernard inserts himself with discretion into the debate over Hildegard. His point of view, so to speak, was to insist as firmly as possible on humility. All that follows merely strengthens this position. Far from judging Hildegard, he has just given her an urgent bit of advice. 'Better still (*ceterum*)', since you have the inner learning and the anointing which teaches all things, what more can we teach or counsel you? According to the first letter of Saint John (2:20,27) and according to tradition, 'the anointing which teaches everything' is none other than the Spirit of God. This text and interpretation were both dear to Bernard: Each of us must interiorize the teaching received from God through the Holy Spirit. Here Bernard draws a contrast between the fact that the Spirit alone teaches everything, and his own inability to teach.

Consequently, having laid his finger on this fact and pointed out the contrast between the power of the Spirit and his own inability, all Bernard could do was pray: 'So here is what we shall do instead . . .'. With words taken from Saint Paul (1 Th 4:1, 2 Th 3:12), he exhorts and begs her to do the same. And then quoting Saint Paul again, 'He asks and beseeches her insistently' to remember before

God him, and all those united to him in spiritual communion. There was absolutely no selfishness on Bernard's
part; he did not attempt to profit by being in contact with a
mystic in the hope of obtaining some personal gain. His
thought was for others and he asked Hildegard to extend to
them the affection she felt for him. Did he have in mind the
community of Clairvaux or the whole cistercian community? He would seem to have been thinking, in the broader
sense of all those men and women who make up a 'spiritual society in the Lord', in whom all are 'united'. This final
word is in keeping with the opening sentence whose first
word was *dilectae*, part of the language of love.

So ends this short note which, given the circumstances—
mystic visions and their role in the Church—could well
have been much more fully developed. It brings the joust
in humility to a halt, for both Hildegard and Bernard were
aware of being rather important people with a role to play.
Bernard, in other letters addressed to churchmen or
leaders in society, was perfectly capable of speaking out as
master, abbot, father, and authoritative advisor. Yet here,
writing to Hildegard, he says he feels himself weak and
lacking enough authority to render judgement. There was
no unconscious tyrannical intrusion into Hildegard's spiritual experience. Bernard respected the working of grace
within her. Was this excessive prudence on his part or a
refusal to get involved? What little he did say surely gives
evidence of a courageous stand: he approved and encour-
aged Hildegard but refrained from going into detail, and
this for a very clear reason: he had neither the competence
nor the required authority. She had asked him to judge. He
replied with a brief bit of generally applicable advice, something which could have been written to anyone. He sent
her back to interiority and humility, which are the only
guarantees of authenticity for any christian experience
manifesting itself outwardly and attracting attention. And
in these few lines he led his correspondent from her own
intimacy of soul to universal communion and he helped
her be led.

Bernard's relations with the abbess of Bingen did not stop there. Shortly after this exchange of letters, towards the end of 1147, Eugene III appointed a commission charged with examining Hildegard's teaching. They went to see her, questioned her, and noticed her humility, the touchstone of holiness. The pope read everything she had already written in the *Scivias* and he had it read at Trier in the presence of Bernard, who admired it greatly. It would seem that his intervention decided Eugene III not only to approve Hildegard, but also to ask her to write down 'everything she might learn from the Holy Spirit', from the anointing Bernard had mentioned in his letter to her.[20] From that time on Hildegard's correspondence with the powerful of this world increased.[21] And so it was that the abbot of Clairvaux effectively defended a woman, to the great joy of many.

---

[20]Russel, 424–425.
[21]A. Führkötter, 130.

# CHAPTER IV

# WISE VIRGINS AND FOOLISH QUEENS

## 1. *A Message for Sophia.*

SEVERAL ENLIGHTENING STUDIES have been devoted to the problem of young people in the society of the twelfth century, and we are, on the whole, better informed about boys than girls. It is therefore all the more important that Bernard took an interest in them. Letter 113 ( VII:287–289) is addressed 'to the virgin Sophia', an unmarried woman living in ordinary society. She belonged to that group of people who, like everyone else, could profit by a programmed routine for the spiritual life and ongoing personal reform. Though he had written for many other social groups, Bernard had until then said nothing to these women. He intended to make up for lost time. There is no indication as to who the recipient may have been, nor can we even be sure that she really existed—her very name, 'Wisdom' in Latin, seems to be symbolic. The same word was used in the Old Testament as one of the divine attributes and even as a name for God himself, with whom we can be united in spiritual espousals.[1] In the gospel parable of the five wise and the five foolish virgins, a contrast is sketched between five prudent, vigilant young women and

---

[1] See R.A. Horsley, 'Spiritual Marriage with Sophia' in *Vigiliae Christianae* 33 (1979) 30–54.

five others, improvident and foolish.[2] Up to our own day Sophia has always been more of a symbol than a reality, or to be more precise, she has been the symbol of a reality: the reality of a life of union with God.[3]

The title Bernard gave Sophia might lead us to expect a treatise on virginity. But, as we shall see, Bernard's main concern here was not that particular state of life, but everything that goes to make up the spiritual 'adornments' of young girls. To do this, Bernard drew a series of contrasts, as he was fond of doing and did so often. Following the Gospel, he pointed out what distinguishes the wise virgins from the others.

Before studying the content of this letter, we need to stress its very literary character. The text as we have it was very carefully reworked over a first and then a second time. The manuscript tradition reveals more than forty-five corrections in the second draft, and another seven in the third. The presence of this letter in the so-called 'short' collection, the one that existed before the register compiled by Geoffrey of Auxerre around 1145, is the single chronological clue that we can uncover.[4] None of the successive textual modifications in any way changed the views Bernard expressed in it. All changes were made with a view to making the text more pleasing to the ear, a change in the order of words, for example, or the use of a more elegant word.[5] A biblical sentence used at the beginning was altered to bring

---

[2]Mt 25: 1–13.

[3]The importance of the theme of *sophia* in the work of Saint Hildegard in the twelfth century has been illustrated by B.L. Grant, 'Hildegard and Wisdom' in *Anima* 61 (1980) 125–129. For our century we need only recall the title of the work by Étienne Gilson, *Les tribulations de Sophie*.

[4]On the successive states—short (B), long (L), and finished (Pf)—of the collection of Saint Bernard's letters, specifics have been given in SBOp VII (Rome, 1974) Introduction, ix–xxii.

[5]For example, at n. 2, p.289, 7, *canitura* has been substituted in L-Pf for *cantatura* in B.

it into line with the text of the Vulgate.[6] This sort of 'bible game', which Bernard was fond of playing, is illustrated by the second word of the letter.[7] Quoting the Book of Proverbs, he uses, instead of the word 'grace' which is in the text, 'glory': in the context of this letter the two words scarcely differ in meaning. In what follows the theme is glory; the word itself and others derived from it[8] recur more than fifteen times. In these four pages we find more than forty-five reminiscences or citations of the Bible and also the liturgy.

Bernard used many stylistic devices: word plays, internal rhymes, assonances, contrasts, sound plays. And these all enhance the text with a musicality which is in itself an illustration of the theme: beauty.[9] Among the various rhetorical devices inherited from antiquity, one in particular was used by Bernard over and over again. It consisted in declaring that the writer will say nothing about the subject he intends to write about: 'I omit. . . I keep quiet. . . I pass over. . . I remain silent. . . I say nothing. . .' (Ep 113.3–4). In composing his letter, Bernard started with discreet and distant allusions leading up to the marriage theme, introduced by a reminiscence of the liturgy for virgins and then clearly stated by an allusion to the Song of Songs, and then finally imposed by means of three quotations from Psalm 44, an epithalamium. In keeping with a device frequently found in Bernard's writings, a well-worked out play on words or an explicit quotation from Scripture, latches on to an earlier word which is picked up and carried forward to be orchestrated later in the text. It is almost as if there were

---

[6]In the second part of v.30 of Proverbs 31, Bernard gave *mulier sapiens*; L and Pf have *mulier timens Deum*, like the Vulgate.

[7]On the liberty with which Bernard, so to speak, played with biblical texts, see *Receuil d'e'tudes sur S. Bernard* III (Rome, 1969) 241–245.

[8]We have *gloriosus* (twice), *gloriari* (twice), *gloriola* (once).

[9]We cite here only a few examples: *fragili et nobili, exponit-deponit, furis calliditas-furentis crudelitas, fugacium-fallacium, tutus quia tuus,* and, in the last line, *de corpore abit, non obit cum corpore.*

some sort of chain reaction going on in Bernard's mind from the subconscious to the fully conscious level.[10] Sometimes we find different devices joined in a single formula. For example, in the first paragraph two biblical words 'pass' (*praeterit*: 1 Co 7:31) and 'dwell' (*manet*: Jn 6:57) are followed by two formulas in which the ideas and sound tones are expressed in perfect parallel: *iucunditas non reditura-anxietas non relictura*, which we might attempt to translate approximately as:

Passing joy ne'er returns,
Dwelling trouble ever turns.

The consonance of *reditura-relictura* includes contrasting meanings: 'never comes again-never ends'; the result is the same in both instances: the absence of joy, the presence of trouble, suggested by the coupling of two different values: *iucunditas* with *praeterit*, and *anxietas* with *manet*. The nub of this word-play is a fairly common intuition: joy cannot abide permanently, whereas unhappiness digs in and settles down. However it is said and done, whether *reditura* or *relictura*, similar in sound but opposite in meaning, the whole situation is unbearable. We could go on analyzing this text without ever exhausting the riches or the subtle refinements of this letter. One thing is certain: Bernard intended giving the young ladies of his day—and of days still to come—a masterpiece. This letter is a jewel.

Now let us turn to the message it contains. Its title could well be 'There is Beauty and beauty'. The very salutation already suggests a potential contrast between virginity as a mere title, and its reality as a state of life: 'To Sophia, virgin: may she retain this title, may she win its fruits'—a

---

[10]For example: in n.1 (288, 5) *certantibus ceteris* prepares *Certent ergo ceterae* (288, 15); in n.2 (289, 14), *spectabilis. . . angelis admirandus ornatus* leads into *speciosi. . . in quem desiderant angeli prospicere* (289, 23; reminiscence of 1 P 1:12); in n.6 (291, 3) *tutus* is taken from line 11 in the word play: *tutus quia tuus*.

gospel phrase meaning its *rewards*.[11] Throughout the text we notice the contrast between outward adornment and the inner person, the transitory and the enduring, the exterior and the interior, the 'fallacious' and illusory and what is firm and true. The initial biblical text, 'Deceptive is grace. . .', has been purposely modified and become 'Deceptive is glory. . .'. The glory of the body, even decked out with precious ornaments, is deceptive; grace along beautifies the soul. Little by little the notion of vainglory, useless glory, fades away to leave room for the only absolute glory: the glory of Christ. Three words describing the beauty of the bride in Psalm 44 are discreetly recalled and made the substance of two whole paragraphs: *decor, pulchritudo, confessio. Confessio* has three different meanings on which Bernard plays, moving imperceptibly from one to the other: the confession by which we recognize our sins and the fact that we are sinners; the confession of praise given to God which we ourselves receive from him; and, finally, beauty itself. Other related words—*speciosus, lumen*— add fresh variations on the theme. Underlying it all is an implicit theology which reveals its complete meaning only in what Bernard says elsewhere about what we might call his 'aesthetics'.[12] But the general lesson he wants to convey in this letter is that a person should remain faithful to the demands of the state in which he, or she, is actually living. Somewhere else Bernard admits that feminine elegance is one of the ways a wife can please her husband, one of the ways she shows her love for him.[13] As for Sophia, she has only to please Jesus Christ.

---

[11]Yves Congar, 'Les laïcs et l'écclésiologie des "ordines" chez les théologiens de XIᵉ et XIIᵉ siècles' in *I laici nella 'societas christiana' dei secoli XI e XII* (Milan, 1968) 88–89, has given a bibliography and examples to which we could add that of Bernard.

[12]'Essais sur l'esthétique de saint Bernard' in *Studi medievali* 9 (1968) 702–705.

[13]See above.

A second idea is introduced at the beginning of the message: the deceptiveness of noble blood. The Church as a whole and monasticism in particular had often become painfully aware of the drawbacks attached to the privilege of belonging to the nobility that reformers always felt obliged to denounce abuses. The aristocracy, as a purely worldly phenomenon, not sanctified by divine grace, can lead only to vanity, if not to oppression.[14] Bernard sided strenuously with this anti-aristocratic reaction: 'virtue is given to very few; very few, I say, especially among nobles. So, according to Saint Paul, God chooses very few of his elect from among aristocrats. He prefers those who are not noble in the eyes of the world.' With remarkable fidelity to the context from which he took the allusion, Bernard reminds us that 'God shows no partiality towards persons'. We find these words quoted in a chapter of the Rule of Saint Benedict where any preference to nobles just because they are nobles is forbidden in the monastery.[15] Bernard adds quickly that if Sophia is able to unite nobility of birth and nobility of virtue, so much the better: this would be dearer to God in that it is rarer: *tanto carius est quanto rarius* (113.1).

The word virginity is used only twice, and the related words virgin and virginal only seven times in all, three for the first, four for the second. More than a commendation of celibacy, we find here praise for spiritual espousals with the only Bridegroom possible for unmarried persons. It is the nuptial theme which guarantees the coherence of the whole message, centered as it is on personal loving union with Christ the King. Everything to do with this union must be interior and profound, in contrast with all that is exterior, apparent, and superficial in human relations.

---

[14]Art. 'Nobilta' in *Dizionario degli Istituti di Perfezione* 6 (1980) col. 311–317. 'Il monachesimo femminile nei secoli XI[e] XII' in *Movimento religioso femminile e franciscanesimo nel sec. XIII* (Assisi, 1981).

[15]'The Problem of Social Class and Christology in Saint Benedict' in *Word and Spirit* 2 (1980) 33–51.

There follows a series of contrasts between what is 'without'(*foris*) and what is 'within' (*intus*). This in turn leads up to a very dense formula summing everything up in a nutshell: anything that delights is within because He who delights us is within: *Intus est quod delectat, quia intus est quem delectat* (113.3). Our delight is in the Lord, in sharing his own beauty.

'Modesty' is mentioned twice as a characteristic of the christian virgin and set in opposition to the artificial elegance with which certain women try to attract attention and admiration. Beauty of this kind is false and unauthentic because it is based on something besides the real person; this is particularly true of clothing made from animal skins, like ermine and squirrel. This satirical theme is as old as literature itself and Bernard writes about it very soberly by comparison with what Saint Jerome had to say on the matter.[16] Bernard devotes two lines to the theme in paragraph two, another two lines in the next paragraph, and makes a few allusions in paragraph five. He holds no tirade, but makes only short and scattered remarks on the subject. Was he hinting at someone in particular, or a certain group of people. Just as his models were presented in scriptural terms—the daughter of Sion or Jerusalem, and her Bridegroom, Christ the King—, so too are the anti-models—the daughter of Belial or Babylon—: mere commonplaces which had no special meaning in the tradition but suggest infidelity to God and his commandments. Once, towards the end, the word 'queen' is used in the plural (113.5), as is the word 'royal' (6). It was the custom in Saint Bernard's day to represent queens dressed in keeping with the elegant fashions of the times, as we see on the west portal of Saint Denis and in other sculptures.[17] And

---

[16]D.S. Wiesen, *Saint Jerome as a Satirist. A Study of Christian Latin Thought and Letters* (Ithaca, 1964).

[17] According to E.S. Greenhill, 'Eleanor, Abbot Suger and Saint Denis' in William W. Kibler, ed., *Eleanor of Aquitaine, Patron and Politician* (Austin-London, 1976) 92–93 and 111.

who more than queens had the required means for buying expensive clothes and finery? These people with biblical names were just as fictitious as the virgin Sophia. Bernard invented them to serve the cause he was preaching. The only theme he developed at length was that of spiritual beauty, because it is more important than any satire on false beauty. Bernard's aim in this letter was to issue an invitation to interiority.

## 2. *Eleanor of Aquitaine: An Awful Example?*

The name of one famous woman never occurs in Bernard's letters: Eleanor of Aquitaine. Yet, if we are to believe certain authors, she was, along with Heloise, one of the most renowned women of her day. As early as the end of the twelfth century, her importance had been amplified by legend to a degree now acknowledged as exaggerated. Even if it is no longer accurate to say that everyone during her lifetime was talking about her—for better or for worse— at least they knew about her. Bernard met her personally at least once. How can we explain his lack of comment? Did he realize her influence was limited? Or, on the contrary, did he see her as the shadow, the anti-model, as it were, of womankind as he liked to envisage it? Faced with the mystery of silence, we can imagine almost anything. And people have. It is worth our while, therefore, to examine carefully what we do know in the light of the original sources.

This is one of those instances where we watch the rise of what might be called historical legends. Unwarranted hypotheses, put forward in an authoritative way, readily take hold and become well established. In our century, even our own day, the learned author most fertile in the field is Amy Kelly. In 1950 she published *Eleanor of Aquitaine and the Four Kings*, a book which has been reprinted numerous times.[18]

---

[18]Amy Kelly, *Eleanor of Aquitaine and the Four Kings* (Cambridge, Mass., 1950). I have used the nineteenth reprint, dated 1979.

Her information is matched by her imagination, and both are well-served by a compelling style. Consequently, her book lies behind a whole series of romantic biographies. The index, at the word *Bernard*, refers the reader to the many pages where he is mentioned as someone involved in every phase of life and all the activities of the leading character, and he is persistently referred to—in the english text—as 'the abbé'.[19]

The tone is set practically at the start in connection with the trial of Abelard in 1140:

> It was about this time, when his fame was at its height, that Abbé Bernard came in contact with Queen Eleanor. Since he avoided palaces and gaudy spectacles that royalty present, he must have encountered her at some public event, very possibly at Sens. Louis was there, and it is not likely that Eleanor denied herself that pilgrimage . . . .[20]

The probability, or the likelihood, of other meetings is then immediately suggested, and throughout the book the psychology of both the monk and the queen are reconstructed:

> Of course, queens were as grass to the abbé. But when he first had sight of Eleanor there must have been a special secular magnificence about her to draw his reluctant eye and his burning words. To whom if not to the queen and her suite does the abbe' allude in that epistle in which he describes the practices of noble ladies to his nuns as an example of all they must take pains to avoid? The passage in some points takes substance from Isaiah's strictures on the harlots of Israel.[21]

---

[19]*Index*, 418.
[20]P. 19.
[21]P. 20.

This is followed by ten lines or so 'adapted' from Bernard's epistle 113, lines composed of freely translated phrases taken from here and there in Bernard's long text and arranged to make up a portrait or, more precisely a caricature, of the elegance of Eleanor and the ladies in her train. And Kelly concludes: 'This makes the abbé's convictions clear. . . .'[22]

From beginning to end, Bernard is depicted as obsessed with this ridiculous image of Eleanor, as this historian is obsessed with the abbé's revulsion for her. Authors who depend on this presentation sometimes tone down the exaggerations. They admit, for example, that the duchess of Aquitaine and the abbot of Clairvaux were in agreement about the second Crusade and that she was his ally in recruiting knights for the expedition.[23] Yet in a recent biography of Eleanor we come across Amy Kelly's words reproduced with almost no modification. At Sens in 1140,

> . . . there must have been something exceptionally magnificent about Eleanor and her ladies-in-waiting. . . He must have watched those exquisites for quite a time. . . . It is ironic that the only surviving physical portrait of Eleanor comes from a man who viewed her as a Babylonian harlot.[24]

And so it goes on: conjectures and hypotheses have become glibly repeated statements.

Another text describing Eleanor of Aquitaine reconstructs feminine fashion of the twelfth century, very different from that of the tenth and the eleventh centuries. The text is illustrated with a reproduction of statues from a

---

[22]P. 21.

[23]Regine Pernoud, *Aliénor d'Aquitaine* (Paris, 1979) 52.

[24]Marion Meade, *Eleanor of Aquitaine. A Biography* (New York, 1977) 65.

portal at Chartres, dating from about 1150:

> It is easy to imagine Eleanor in the guise of one of the
> queens of Judah.... The pious, ascetic abbot was
> shocked... by Eleanor's proud femininity and love of
> display. He wrote an epistle to the nuns of his Cister-
> cian order in which he warned them against the per-
> nicious example of fashionable ladies....[25]

The author is referring to letter 113, written to young
Sophia, and he goes on to give, with no indication of the
source, the usual extracts containing what little Bernard
had to say about the way ladies dressed.

Happily, the fictional aspect of these reconstructions
born of fertile imaginations has now been detected.[26] Even
so, we still read statements like this:

> Bernard's opinion of her—he considered her to be the
> evil genius behind some of the king's more unsavory
> actions—and of women in general certainly did not
> alleviate her feelings of being a *mal-mariée*.[27]

This is how one opinion influences others. It is high time
we get down to asking the documents themselves what
they say, no more, no less.

Bernard never wrote to Eleanor, but he sent six letters to
her husband, Louis VII.[28] In not one of these letters does he
so much as mention her. We might think he did not dare
attack her directly. Yet he never hesitated to address the

---

[25]Claude Marks, *Pilgrims, Heretics and Lovers. A Medieval Journey* (New
York, 1975) 135–136.

[26]'In many instances various parts of this work [Kelly, *Eleanor*] come
very close to fiction and romance and rest on fragile literary and historical evidence', Moshe' Lazar, 'Cupid, the Lady and the Poet' in Kibler,
(see n.17) 11.

[27]*Ibid.*, 39. The idea and phrase of 'evil genius' are repeated in Meade,
66, as are those about 'Bernard's personal hostility towards the queen',
148.

[28]Epp 170, 220, 221, 226, 283, 303.

king in harsh words, reproaching him, for example, from one end to the other of the long letter 221.[29] Surely, if he had had anything to say to the queen, he would not have fallen back on doing it anonymously by means of a message to some unknown maiden in letter 113. Similarly, Bernard vehemently denounced the king's misdeeds in a long letter to cardinal Stephen, without the slightest allusion to his queen. In the last paragraph of this letter he mentions, among other instances of marriages marred by consanguinity, the union between Louis and Eleanor. But he lay no particular stress on it.[30] And, again, whenever Bernard wrote to Suger about the king, he mentioned only him.[31]

It has often been said that the presence of Eleanor and other 'amazons' on the second crusade was one of the causes of its failure. At the beginning of Book II of the *De consideratione*, where Bernard indulged in a retrospective examination of conscience about this disaster, he attributed it, not to the presence of women, of whom there is no mention, but to division between christian princes (Csi II.1–4).

Let us look for a moment at the only document which relates the interview Bernard had with Eleanor at Saint-Denis in 1144. Shortly after the event, Geoffrey of Auxerre inserted an account of it into the *Fragmenta* he had compiled in preparation for a biography of Saint Bernard. This is the only reliable text we have. It reads as follows:

> Here is what happened on the feast of blessed Denis, in the church of this same martyr. Queen Eleanor was talking with our Father [Bernard], lamenting the fact that, as the Bible puts it, God had closed her womb.

---

[29]Ep 221; VIII: 84–86; in 1143.

[30]Ep 224; VIII: 91–93; in 1144.

[31]Ep 377, 381; VIII: 340–341, 345–346: in 1149 and about 1150.

She had been living with the king for almost nine
years. In the first years, it is true, she did conceive but
she had a miscarriage and since then had remained
barren. She was now beginning to despair of becoming a mother. As she was lamenting about this
piteously, the venerable Father said to her 'Try confidently to achieve peace and I, confident of God's
mercy, promise you children'. The queen told the
king about this. When peace had been made he sent
secretly for the blessed man, asking him to keep the
promise he had made to the queen. Far from going
back on his promise, he confidently repeated the
promise that this would soon come to pass. And in
fact, that same year, the queen conceived and gave
birth to a child. Immediately after the birth, she sent
someone post-haste to announce the news to the man
of God and to thank him. We know, in fact, that she
had conceived at approximately the same time peace
had been made, as is evident from the date of the
birth.[32]

A few years later, while writing book IV of the *Vita prima*
of Bernard, Geoffrey of Auxerre inserted a new version of
the same events and it too is worth quoting:

The queen of France, wife of Louis the Young, had
lived with him for several years without having a
child. Now, the holy man [Bernard] was with the
king, working at some peace treaty to which the
queen was opposed. As he was advising her to give
up her schemes and suggest better things to the king,
in the course of the conversation she began to lament
her barrenness and humbly asked Bernard to obtain

---

[32]R. Lechat, ed., 'Les Fragmenta de vita et miraculis sancti
Bernardi, par Geoffroy d'Auxerre' in *Analecta Bollandiana* 50 (1932)
118, n.55.

from God that she give birth. He answered her saying 'If you follow my advice, then I too will pray for what you ask'. She consented and peace was soon established. When this had happened, the king, at the queen's suggestion, humbly asked the man of God to keep his promise. And this he did so quickly that the following year, about the same date, the queen had a child.[33]

In the two versions of this event the account is restrained but suggestive. In the first place we should note that it is quite in keeping with the twelfth-century idea that a wife's influence on her husband should be exerted during the intimacies of married life; it was then that she could get him to change his mind or turn him from his errant ways. So Bernard was teaching Eleanor how to go about things in a good pastoral way.[34] According to the text—the only one written by a contemporary, perhaps even an eye-witness— the interview was not stormy; both parties were on good terms. They came easily to an agreement and it was Eleanor who adopted Bernard's opinion without any resistance. The queen, growing confident in the course of the conversation (*inter loquendum*) presented her request 'with humility'. And he knew how to handle the matter without giving offense.

---

[33]*Vita prima Sancti Bernardi* IV.18, *PL* 185: 332. On the date of this text and what it relates, see A.H. Bredero: 'Etudes sur le "Vita Prima" de saint Bernard' in *Analecta S.O.C.* 17 (1961) 220–221, n.11. This passage was later suppressed in the second draft of the *Vita prima*: Bredero, *Analecta* 18 (1962) 28–29. Suppressions of this kind were made to avoid mentioning persons who were still living at the time when an attempt was being made to get the pope to canonize Bernard, according to Bredero, *Bernhard von Clairvaux im Widerstreit der Historie* (Wiesbaden, 1966) 40–43.

[34]In *Monks and Marriage. A Twelfth Century View* (New York, 1982) I have given samples.

A recent book devoted to Eleanor argues that successive authors of the persistent legends about her aimed simply to 'sully Eleanor'[35] and 'dirty her face'.[36] The abbot of Clairvaux made no contribution to the job.

---

[35] J. Markale, *La vie, la légende et l'influence d'Aliénor, comtesse de Poitou, duchesse d'Aquitaine, Reine de France puis d'Angleterre, Dame des Troubadours et des Bardes bretons* (Paris, 1979) 196 and 211.

[36]*Ibid.*, 209. On the relations between Bernard and Eleanor, the most balanced pages are still those of E.R. Lalande, 'Pour une image véridique d'Aliénor d'Aquitaine' in *Bulletin de la Sociéte' des Antiquaires de l'Ouest et Musées de Poitiers* (1952) 179–180 and 195.

# CHAPTER V

# MASCULINE AND FEMININE ACCORDING TO SAINT BERNARD

*1. Differentiated Equality between the Sexes.*

D OES WOMAN, WE MAY ASK, possess less value than man? In her relationship with God, is she inferior to him?

There is no demeaning prejudice in Bernard's writings. He says nothing *a priori* about woman and takes nothing as a foregone conclusion, independently of what he received from his, basically biblical, christian culture. Everything he had to say about the differences between man and woman was based, as was almost everything else, on scriptural texts or their resonances. He borrowed a few formulas and examples from the Old Testament and these are, to all intents and purposes, favorable or unfavorable in equal proportion. Most of the texts he used, however, came from the New Testament, and more frequently from the Gospels than from the letters of Saint Paul or other books. And here, even if we leave aside the praises of the Virgin Mary, the majority of the texts he refers to are favorable to women. Eve he generally excused. He never reproached her unduly or considered that she alone was to blame for the many woes that have befallen humanity, as do certain authors of every epoch, including Bernard's own twelfth century. On the subject of her guilt he proposes an authentic and remarkably delicate theology.

Like every other writer from Antiquity onward, Bernard
was acquainted with the theme of the 'weaker sex'.[1] He did
not overuse it, and in the only three cases where he did use
it, he retained the original meaning—a lesser physical
strength, somewhat akin to the weaker strength of youth
as compared with that of adulthood: he says so clearly in a
letter in which he congratulates a young nun on overcom-
ing the double weakness of 'a fragile sex and age'.[2] The
formula he used comes from the liturgy, where it is used in
praise of women who show courage in the face of martyr-
dom and in other circumstances. Elsewhere, in addressing
men, Bernard used the comparative and spoke of the 'more
fragile sex',[3] or the 'weaker sex'.[4] Only once, with the
intention of humiliating prelates who dressed like women,
did he mention the sex and 'order' or social category which
is, by comparison, 'baser'.[5] But to speak like that in those
times was the accepted thing.

In four other places, using a traditional formula, Bernard
brought together three criteria distinguishing persons: sex,
age, and social standing. But he also stated that this introduces no inequality in matters of salvation: neither Saint
Paul nor Saint Malachy heeded them: they, like the salvation of which they were the ministers, were both accessible
to everyone, men and women.[6] On that beautiful page in
the *Apologia*, where Bernard sings the praises of conciliation between diversity and unity in the Church, he says
that this is a mystery appealing to both sexes, to every age
and social condition.[7] Lastly, when, towards the end of his

---

[1]Witnesses are cited in *Thesaurus linguae latinae* VI.1 (Leipzig, 1912–
1926) col. 1228, and in K. Thraede, art. 'Frau' in *Reallexicon für Antike und
Christentum* VIII (Stuttgart, 1972) col. 242–269.

[2]Ep 114.1; VII:292, 8.

[3]Ep 42.6; VII:105–22.

[4]SC 71.4; II:216, 24.

[5]Ep 42.4; VII:104, 7.

[6]D 96.3; VI.1:357, 18; Mal 3; VI/1:52, 10

[7]Apo 6; III:87, 2.

life, he devoted one of his sermons on the Song of Songs to refuting the Rhineland heretics, he spoke in the same way of the 'diversity between the sexes': Saint Paul bestows a 'great blessing'[8] on widows who remarry, while heretics segregate the sexes.[9]

Apart from the rare allusions to the 'weaker sex' which we have just mentioned, very few negative statements, unfavorable to women, are to be found in Bernard's works. We found only three of them above,[10] and even these are couched in biblical terms. Furthermore, in the Bible these allusions had a stronger meaning, while Bernard's use was tempered by the context in which he set them.[11] He was careful never to stress the point. Far from condemning or humiliating woman, he tended more to exalt her, even to idealize her, as was the tendency perhaps in certain romances of his day. But worldly authors exalted women in a different way and for different reasons. As is usual with people who are happy in their celibate state, he easily overlooked certain concrete aspects of ordinary relationships between men and women.

## 2. *Mary, a Symbol of Feminine Qualities.*

Now we must inquire whether—as is sometimes maintained—Bernard did not, by exalting the Virgin Mary, idealize woman, projecting her image beyond the real world. The purpose of the present study is not to deal with his mariology as a whole. This has already, not very long ago, been done in a conclusive manner.[12] All we need do

---

[8] SC 66.4–5; II:180–181.

[9] SC 66.8; II:183, 28.

[10] See above, chapter one, note 16; Ep 42, quoted above; 1 Sent. III (SBOp VI/2:110) quoted above.

[11] See *Monks and Love...* , 44–47.

[12] Everything essential has been said with all the necessary nuances and specifics, with exhaustive documentation, by H. Barré, 'Saint Bernard, docteur marial' in *Saint Bernard théologien, Analecta S.O.C.* IX, 3–4 (1953) 92–113. Father Olivar has given an excellent summary in his

here is examine the attention he gave to what we might—using his own word—call woman's condition.

Bernard wrote on this in his early work, *Homilies in Praise of the Virgin Mother*. In answer to the rather skeptical question attributed to Solomon, 'Who shall find a valiant woman?' Bernard affirmed the dignity of woman, in spite of the limits inherent in her condition: 'The wise man was well acquainted with the weakness of this sex, frail in body and fickle in mind'. But Bernard had also read in the Book of Genesis the promise God made to woman, that 'he who had prevailed over woman would in turn be prevailed over by her'. The first thing we should notice, then, is that 'the salvation of us all, the restitution of our innocence, and victory over the enemy are all in the hands of a woman'. Consequently, this woman must of necessity be valiant, capable of assuming such a task. Any worth she may have, 'her price', can only come from heaven, from God himself. This woman will be none other than Mary, the child-bearing virgin who did not suffer the pains of childbirth. [13]

That it is necessary for a woman to share in the work of salvation was one of Bernard's firm convictions. We come across it again in his *Sermon for the Sunday within the Octave of the Assumption*. [14] The equality between man and woman, and their complementarity in diversity, is such that the first sin was committed by both, though more gravely by man than by woman. Reparation needs, then, to be made by both man and woman and, here again, it is man who has the major part to play. Everything could have been done by Christ alone: 'He sufficed'. But it was good for us that, side by side with this new Adam, there should be a new Eve. Both sexes had to be represented in the work of salvation. And what particular aspect of human nature was the new

---

introduction to *San Bernardo de Claravel; San Amadeo de Lausana, Homilias marianas* (Buenos Aires, 1980) 19–48.

[13] Miss 2.5; IV:24.

[14] O Asspt., 1–2; V:262–263. Nuanced commentary in Barré, 98–100.

Eve to stress? Here we notice a progression in Bernard's thought. Since Christ is 'majesty', wielding the power to judge, we might well have feared him had he been alone. Woman acts as the intermediary between him and us. Two pithy, assonant, sentences, express the exact parallel between 'cruel Eve', and 'faithful Mary'. Through the first the ancient enemy poured a plague virus into man; by the second both man and woman received the antidote. But in each case woman was the servant, *ministra*. Yet her very presence and her intervention are enough to allay all fear. In her we see, not something terrible, but gentleness, a capacity for self-giving and universal oblation: *omnibus offerens*. According to the Gospel Mary never said anything reproachful, never a hard word, nor did she show the slightest sign of indignation. Everything in her is full of pity, grace, pardon, and goodness. And it is in this sense that she is an 'infinitely kind mediatrix'. She opens up her bosom of mercy to all so that of her fullness all may receive. She has something to offer every human person without exception: she comforts and consoles prisoners, the sick, the sad, sinners and righteous alike. She is the joy of the angels and, the glory of the Trinity, and she gives her own substance to the Person of the Son. All that we may hope to receive from her comes from her nature and her qualities as a woman.

Bernard sometimes pondered how she could possess such power and such fervor in so frail a nature. It is because the Holy Spirit had come upon her: hence her 'familiar, close, intimate union with Christ', not on the sentimental level, but solely by the fact that they were united in a single flesh, while remaining infinitely different.[15] The unique manner in which God was present in her explains her effacement, her modesty in relationship to the apostles and their rivalries.[16] Her kindness, her compassion, her charity

---

[15]O Asspt., 5, pp. 265–266.
[16]*Ibid.*, 11, p. 271.

all flowed from her humility. She is 'Mother of mercy'.[17] Hers is not to pardon, but as the mother of him who can pardon, she places herself between us and the majesty of both God and Christ, whose godhead might otherwise frighten us.[18]

In such texts, Bernard mentions the awesome and distant nature of Christ simply for rhetorical purposes, to make more persuasive his plea in favor of Mary. Everywhere else, he insists, to the contrary, on the fact that by his loving and imitable humanity Christ is very close to us, ever ready to welcome and forgive us.

The theme of the necessity of the feminine in the work of salvation recurs in one of the final sermons on the Song of Songs. Throughout his earthly life Jesus took pleasure in the company of Martha and Mary. In their presence his heart and mind found rest, and he was comforted by these women's virtues. How wonderful that he, in all his majesty, loved the familiarity of these pure souls and chaste bodies, even though they were only earthly beings, members of the weaker sex. He gave courage to their shyness, joy to their humility, nourishment to their devotion.[19] The pleasure that Jesus took in the feminine sex was a sign of his own humility and his ability to forgive. Thenceforth the Son of God has never ceased coming into this world. Yet he manifests himself, not with power, as the one who is to judge the world, but as he once appeared, 'like a little child, born for us of this feminine, this weaker, sex'. That he should be born of a woman is a sign of his goodness, of his will to forgive, of the gentleness he will show on the day of his wrath.[20] These qualities are not found only in women, but, according to Bernard, it is in women that they are more frequently seen. Even the weakness of their sex is

---

[17]*Ibid.*, 15, p. 274.
[18]Nat BMV, 7; V:279.
[19]SC 71.4; II:216, 17–24.
[20]SC 71.4; II:235.

a natural fact which, though not recognized as a positive value by literary and philosophical tradition, is transformed in Mary, and changed into a symbol of salvation.

His insistence on the presence of feminine qualities, through Mary, in the mystery of Christ and our relations with him, is probably the only really original contribution Saint Bernard made to mariology. Not that he invented Mary's role in the birth of Christ, but he presented it and its consequences in a way which seems to have been largely unique to him and to have expressed his reaction to the culture around him. It is as though in a violent society where men exercised physical and material force, he saw a need for a compensating non-violence, something he attributed to women, and particularly to Mary. The two kinds of equality he saw in her were the opposites of the failings for which women were generally reproached. On the one hand, women were supposed to lack courage because they were weak; that was why Bernard was fond of quoting Solomon's 'valiant woman'. On the other hand, traditional misogyny reproached women with being arrogant, moody, and shrewish, talkative and fond of spicy gossip. Bernard believed that women—Martha, Mary her sister, and the Virgin Mary—were capable of calmness and kindness and holding their tongues: he praised the Virgin's silence.[21] She is not the only woman to have these qualities; they are found in others as well. But in her, the Mother of God, they are present perfectly and symbolically.

Everything Bernard said about Mary, including her virtues, was already found in Scripture as the patristic and liturgical tradition had interpreted it for him.[22] All Bernard did was to set to music in unequalled magnificence of language a few texts which were the common property of the whole Church. Perhaps he did fall victim to his

---

[21]On the silence of Mary, see Nat BMV, 10–12; V:281–283.
[22]On the sources, see Barré, 108–112.

own literary talent and therefore exaggerated his themes slightly. But he never considered Mary apart from Jesus and his mysteries, on the one hand, nor, on the other, did he set her apart from the humanity Christ redeemed. Because of the perfection of his style, the intensity of his sentiments, the beauty of his teaching, Bernard's ideas were soon taken up by other writers who either developed or diminished them. Many of the exaggerations for which he has sometimes been criticized are to be found in apocryphal writings, often of late origin ascribed to him, and it is these which have sometimes inspired a literature and an iconography for which Bernard should in no way be held responsible.

### 3. *A Woman in Power: The Queen Mother*

Do the feminine qualities which Bernard recognized in Mary have to do solely with compassion? Do they show up simply the natural attitudes any mother would have for her children? Or can we detect in them other activities generally associated with men, but ones which biblical and secular literary traditions have demonstrated can be found in women too? To find the answer to this query, let us examine carefully just one text in Bernard's writings.

#### 'MARY THE QUEEN' IN THE SERMONS OF SAINT BERNARD

We find very few prayers in the writings of Saint Bernard. And yet there is a very beautiful concentrated prayer which is still recited in common every day in certain benedictine monasteries. It is found at the end of his Second Sermon for Advent.[23] It helps us bring together several aspects of the vocabulary the abbot of Clairvaux used in speaking about the Blessed Virgin. Many of his expressions are biblical. Other words he borrowed from the language of law and feudalism. To prove this we have only to

---

[23]De adv., II.5.

comment on the several words of the prayer and compare them with formulas found in other marian pages written by Bernard. First, let us attempt to give a translation of this invocation to provide a starting point for our inquiry.[24]

> Our Lady,
> our mediatrix,
> our advocate,
> to your Son, reconcile us,
> to your Son, commend us,
> to your Son, present us.
> Obtain,
> O Blessed lady,
> by the grace found in you,
> by the privilege deserved by you,
> by the Mercy born of you,
> that he who,
> by your mediation,
> deigned to share our infirmity
> and our misery,
> may, by your intercession,
> let us also share his glory
> and his blessedness,
> he, Jesus Christ,
> your Son,
> our Lord,
> blessed above all
> for ever and ever.

---

[24]The latin text follows. The juridical words appear in italics: *Domina* nostra, *mediatrix* nostra, *advocata* nostra, tuo Filio nos *reconcilia*, tuo Filio nos *commenda*, tuo Filio nos *repraesenta*. Fac, o benedicta, per *gratiam* quam invenisti, per *praerogativam* quam meruisti, per misericordiam quam peperisti, ut qui, te mediante, fieri dignatus est particeps infirmitatis et miseriae nostrae, te quoque intercedente participes faciat nos gloriae et beatitudinis suae, Iesus Christus Filius tuus, Dominus noster . . . For *peperisti*, Mabillon (PL 183:43C,l.4) gives the variant *percepisti*, a weak, derived lesson. This is not substantiated by the manuscripts.

Let us take a few of these words, one by one, and try to define them more precisely. As we shall see, some enunciate Mary's titles, others her functions.

## Mary's Titles

**OUR LADY**: the latin word used here—*domina*—is to be taken in its strongest meaning, as it was used in the Middle Ages. The masculine equivalent, *dominus*, was the lord, the master, the person who possessed and exercised domination and lordship. Just as Jesus is Lord and King, so Mary is lady and queen, because she is the mother of the Lord, the mother of the King. This entitles her to be 'queen of the world'.[25] Mary is queen because her son is King. 'Our queen's diadem'[26] is lit up with twelve stars and Bernard invites us to contemplate the 'queen wearing the diadem with which her Son crowned her'.[27] Sharing his glory, she is 'raised upon a royal throne'.[28] We are her serfs (*servuli*) and she is our 'gracious queen'.[29]

**OUR MEDIATRIX**: Mary has a double right to this title. First because she is the means, the path, by which Christ was given and born to us. Bernard used a phrase which is difficult to translate because it contains an allusion to the biblical and patristic theme of the royal road,[30] (the king's highway in the Revised Standard Version): *Virgo regia ipsa est via per quam Salvator advenit.*[31] The Virgin is the road by

---

[25]'*Mundi regina*', Asspt I.4; V:230, 20; '*Regina mundi*', *ibid.*, IV.1; 244, 21.

[26]'*Reginae nostrae diadema*', O Asspt 7; V:267, 9.

[27]'Videte *reginam* in diademate quo coronavit eam Filius suus', *ibid.*, 6; 266, 19–20.

[28]'. . . jam tunc in *regali* solio supra omnes caelestium ordinum legiones exaltatam. . .', *ibid.*, 8: 268, 4–5.

[29]'*Regina clemens*', Asspt IV.9; 250, 13.

[30]On this theme I have given indications under the title 'La voie royale', in *Suppl. de la Vie spirituelle* (November 1948) 339–352, and in *The Love of Learning and the Desire for God* (New York: Fordham, 1977) 297–98.

[31]Adv II.5; IV:174.

which the Saviour came to us, but she is also the means, the path, by which we are to go to Christ. Here again Bernard uses a scriptural reminiscence: 'Through you we have access to the Son, who through you came down to our misery'.[32]

Mary is also mediatrix because she is the intermediary who powerfully intervenes on our behalf before her Son: *potens est enim*.[33] The mediator's role is to conciliate and reconcile. In the language of ancient roman law the mediator is the 'go-between' who tries to settle a dispute and bring about a reconciliation between two parties.[34] In medieval law the word applied to someone who negotiated peace, or to the arbitrator in a lawsuit, or again, the man who stands as warrant, the privileged witness.[35]

We invoke Mary as Mother of 'mercy', in the old french meaning of the word. The latin word *misericordia* means not only mercy, but also the clemency, benevolence, and kindness that a judge may show when passing sentence.[36] After having reminded us that the Church receives life from Christ just as the moon receives light from the sun,[37] Saint Bernard addresses our Lord saying, 'And now the Mother

---

[32]'Per te accessum habeamus [cf. Rom 5:2, Eph 2:18, 3:12] ad Filium. . . ut per te nos suscipit qui per te datus est nobis', Adv II.5; 174, 10–11.

[33]O Asspt 5; 265, 17–18.

[34]'Conciliator, qui se medium inter aliquos dissidentes interposuit ad lites componendas', see A. Forcellini, *Totius latinitatis lexicon* (Padua, 1721) III 47, at the word *Mediator*.

[35]Cf. *Novum glossarium mediae latinitatis*: ed. F. Blatt, *Meabitis-Miles* (Copenhagen, 1961) 292–293.

[36]See *ibid.*, *Miles-Mozytia* (Copenhagen, 1963) 609. On the equivalence of *misericordia*, *merces*, and *mercy*, cf. du Cange, ed. Favre, *Glossarium* (Niort, 1885) V:351, at the word *Merces*.

[37] On this traditional theme I have quoted texts on Saint Bernard and other medieval authors under the title 'Symbolique chrétienne de la lune', in *Lunaires* (Paris, 1947) 133–148. On the patristic sources, see Hugo Rahner, 'Mysterium lunae. Ein Beitrag zur Kirchentheologie der Väterzeit' in *Zeitschrift für katholische Theologie* 63 (1939) 311–349, 428–442; 64 (1940) 61–80, 121–131.

of Mercy, at whose feet the moon lies prostrate, calls upon
you by devout supplications, you who have appointed her
mediatrix—that is to say intermediary, means of communication—before you, O Sun of Justice, with whom she
pleads on our behalf.[38] We entrust ourselves to our Lady so
that 'mercy' may triumph over 'justice'.[39] She intervenes
for us by her prayers, 'attaining the inaccessible majesty by
knocking, asking, seeking'.[40]

  OUR ADVOCATE: the advocate, or better still the ac-
knowledger, to use the word related to the medieval french
*avoue'*, is the person who defends and protects someone
weaker than himself.[41] In the antiphon for Terce in the
Office of Saint Victor, Bernard applies to her the title
'faithful advocate' in a context suggesting law and combat,
and he mentions captives, an athlete, and the person who
exercises the right of patronage; he also speaks of victory
and aid, in the strong sense of the latin word *adiutorium*.[42]
Elsewhere Bernard discusses Jesus' visit to the home of
Martha and Mary, and shows how the Lord defended
Mary against the pharisee and against her sister who
seemed, as it were, to go to law against her. Mary did not
defend herself, nor did she attack Martha: 'Where do you

---

[38]'Jam te, Mater *misericordiae*. . . tuis jacens provoluta pedibus luna,
*mediatricem* sibi apud solem *iustitiae* constitutam. . . *interpellat*', O Asspt
15; 274, 11–12.

[39]Cf. James 2:13: 'Superexaltat autem misericordia iudicium', quoted
in *Sancti Benedicti Regula* 64.10.

[40]'. . . Inaccessam attingit *maiestatem*. . . pulsando, petendo, quar-
endo. . .', Nat BVM 5; V:278:2–3.

[41]Cf. *Mittellateinisches Wörterbuch*, I, 2 (Munich, 1960) col. 266–268. On
the role of the *advocati*, also called *defensores*, see J. Riedmann, 'Vescovi e
avvocati' in *I poteri temporali dei vescovi in Italia e in Germania nel Medioevo*,
a cura di C.G. Mor -H. Schmidlinger (Bologna, 1979) 35–76.

[42]'Nomen tuum et memoriale tuum, Victor, favus distillans in labiis
*captivorum*. Eia ergo, fortis *athleta*, dulcis *patrone*, *advocate fidelis*, exsurge
in *adiutorium* nobis, ut de plena victoria glorieris', SBOp III:507. On this
text see 'Saint Bernard ècrivain d'aprés l'office de saint Victor', in *Revue
bénédictine* 74 (1964) 161.

read that Mary pleads for herself?' (*ubi legis Mariam caus-antem?*).[43] Jesus is her advocate: *Vide praerogativam Mariae, quae in omni causa habeat advocatum.*[44]

It is in this specific sense that Bernard calls the Virgin Mary our advocate. The title suits her in the first place because we are exiles here below: 'We have no lasting city but we are searching for that place where blessed Mary arrived today' by her assumption into heaven.[45] If we are 'enrolled as citizens (*conscripti cives*) of this city [notice the juridical precision of the term] it is very fitting that even in our exile, even by the waters of Babylon, we should remember her.'[46] Here Bernard uses the vocabulary of exile. In this, our miserable state, Mary can act as our advocate because she is the queen-mother, consequently the mother of Mercy—*Advocatam praemisit peregrinatio nostra.*[47] *Peregrinatio* means exile.[48] We are far from God, but our humanity is already in the homeland, near God; it is preceded by our advocate who is none other than the mother of the Judge. She is used to intervening, by right, on our behalf, as 'mother of mercy'; as *mater misericordiae* she is filled with mercy. Thus she is empowered to deal with the matter and negotiate our salvation: *suppliciter et efficaciter salutis nostrae negotia pertractabit.*[49] Finally, she is the mother of God's only Son.[50] Bernard loved word plays, opposing misery

---

[43]Asspt III.2; 239:20–21.

[44]*Ibid.*, lines 25–26.

[45]'. . .nec nobis est manens *civitas*, sed eam inquirimus, ad quam hodie Maria benedicta pervenit', Asspt I.1; 229, 7–8. Before this Bernard had spoken of our complaint—*querela*, another juridical word.

[46]'In qua si *conscripti cives* sumus, dignum profecto est etiam in *exsilio*, etiam super flumina Babylonis, eius recordari', Asspt I.1; 229, 7–11.

[47]*Ibid.*, 15.

[48]On this vocabulary (*exsilium, peregrinatio*) I have done research published in the the book *Aux sources de la spiritualité occidentale* (Paris, 1964) 40–44.

[49]'Quae tamquam *Iudicis* mater, et mater *misericordiae*, suppliciter et efficaciter salutis nostrae *negotia* pertractabit, Asspt I.1; 229:15–16.

[50]'*Regina* caelorum est, misericors est; denique mater est unigeniti Filii Dei', Asspt I.2; 229, 21–22.

(*miseria*) to mercy (*misericordia*), and so contrasting our state as wretched, miserable serfs (*miseri, servuli, miseria nostra*) with Mary's condition, *misericordiae*: 'may our misery have recourse to her mercy.'[51]

Since Mary, queen mother and mother of mercy, is our advocate, sure of gaining a hearing in the presence of the Judge, her Son, what have we to fear? 'Are you afraid of drawing near to the Father? He has given you Jesus as a mediator, and will listen to him out of respect for him. . . . Do you want an advocate in his presence? Have recourse to Mary: she will be given a hearing out of respect for her. Therein lies all my confidence.'[52]

All this shows that Bernard knew what he wanted to say, and he chose the words best suited to the person he was talking about: he called Mary lady, mediatrix, and advocate because each title carried a precise, rich meaning, a meaning he either explained or supposed known. Let us now look at some of the ways in which Mary acts in keeping with these titles.

## MARY'S INTERVENTIONS

In the prayer we are considering, we find Mary's interventions mentioned immediately after her titles. Each of the three titles has a corresponding function and all three are described in juridical terms.

*RECONCILE US*: we have already seen that the mediator's role is to conciliate and the advocate's to reconcile, to

---

[51]'Nos quidem *servuli* tui. . . sed *misericordia* miseris sapit dulcis. . .ut tua quoque *misericordia* plena sit omnis terra. . .Ad hunc *misericordiae* cumulum tota sollicitudine miseria nostra *recurrat*', Asspt IV.8–9; 249, 18–250, 7.

[52]'Ad Patrem verebaris accedere. . . Iesum dedit tibi *mediatorem*. . . Exaudietur utique pro reverentia sua [Heb 5:7], *Advocatum* habere vis et ad ipsum? Ad Mariam *recurre*. . .ex audietur et ipsa pro rèverentia sua. Haec mea maxima fiducia. . .' Nat BMV 7; 279, 11–21. On *recurrere* and *recursus*, see Niermeyer, *Mediae latinitatis lexicon minus* 10 (Leiden, 1963) 894.

make peace between opponents in a lawsuit. Mary can do this because she is the sovereign lady (*domina*). The cause of dissent between God and us is sin: we are sinners, God is holy; and we are opposed to him.

In classical Latin, to reconcile meant to make peace, to conciliate opponents; to reinstate one party into the good graces of another; to restore friendly relations. Cicero more than once brings together the notion of grace and reconciliation. He says, for example, 'to reconcile to grace' (*in gratiam reconciliari*) and uses other similar formulas.[53] In the Church this vocabulary was applied to the forgiveness of sins, to purification rites. We speak, for example, of the reconciliation of penitents; churches and altars are 'reconciled' after having been desecrated.[54] All this shows the need to restore between God and his creature the friendship that had been broken off by enmity.

Bernard applied this terminology to the mystery of the Incarnation. In his first sermon for the Annunciation he reminds us of the 'conflict between the daughters of God'; the lawsuit which he, like other medieval authors, imagined went on among the divine attributes about man.[55] Justice and Mercy have a 'quarrel', 'a great controversy', a 'complicated discussion', an 'altercation', a 'lawsuit'.[56] Finally reconciled, these two daughters of God come to an agreement:[57] 'Justice and Peace kiss each other' (*Justitia et Pax osculatae sunt*).[58] The result is the establishment of an

---

[53]Texts are quoted in R. Stephanus (Estienne), *Thesaurus linguae latinae* (Basle, 1743) vol. IV: 66.

[54]Texts in du Cange, VII: 752–753.

[55]Cf. 'Nouveau témoin du "Conflit des filles de Dieu"' in *Revue bénédictine* 58 (1948) 53–72.

[56]'Verba *quaerimoniae*. . . grandis *controversia*. . . intricata *disceptatio*. . . *altercatio*. . . *contentio*. . .' Ann I.11; V: 25, 8–26,6

[57]'*Reconciliatas* in osculo. . .', *ibid.*, 9; 22,2.

[58]'. . . tunc *iustitia* et *pax* osculatae sunt [Ps 84:11], quae non modice videbantur dissidere', *ibid.*, 14; 29, 1–2.

'unbreakable treaty of friendship'[59] between God and man.

It was Mary who was chosen to bring about this reconciliation. From roman law[60] feudal law adopted the word 'restoration.'[61] It meant reparation for harm done[62] and compensation, just as we speak today of making restitution, with damages and interest. Saint Bernard suggested this by formulas like 'Everything will be restored (*restaurantur*) and with no small interest in graces—*nec sine magno fenore gratiarum.*[63] *Fenus* means the gain, the profit, the interest on money lent.[64] It suggests that we have practised usury: God restores to us more than is required by strict justice. Mercy has won the battle with Justice.[65] Moreover, the Incarnate Son of God retains his judicial power[66] but he uses it to grant us pardon. Mary plays a part in this great work of reconciliation. As Eve was the mediatrix between Adam and the devil, the blessed Virgin is the mediatrix between sinful man and Christ. Full of mercy, this mediatrix opened to all the bosom of mercy (*misericordiae sinum*).[67] The latin word *sinus* means the fold in the upper

---

[59]'siquidem iustitia et pax osculatae sunt, et indissolubile amicitiarum iniere foedus', *ibid.*, 29, 9–10. In the first authentic draft of this sermon, given among the variants in SBOp IV: 28–29 of the edition of the works of Saint Bernard, the *conflictus* is even more vividly dramatized than in the draft so far quoted; the virtues or attributes of God deliberate at length in God's tribunal.

[60]Cf. Stephanus, IV: 69.

[61]Cf. Du Cange, VII: 154.

[62]'Reparatio damni', *ibid.*, 155.

[63]O Asspt 1; 262, 7.

[64]Cf. *Thesaurus linguae latinae*, VI, 1 (Leipzig, 1912- 1926) 481–484.

[65]'Sed, gratias Deo, per unum nihilominus virum et mulierem unam omnia *restaurantur*, nec sine magno *fenore gratiarum*. Neque enim sicut *delictum*, ita et *donum*; sed excedit *damni aestimationem beneficii* magnitudo', O Asspt 1: 262, 6–7.

[66]'Habet tamen et *iudiciariam potestatem*. . .', *ibid.*, ll. 18–19.

[67]. . . invenietur equidem locus eius [Mariae] in hac *reconciliatione*. Opus est enim *mediatore ad mediatorem*. . . Crudelis nimium *mediatrix* Eva. . ., sed *fidelis* Maria. . ., plena mansuetudinis et *misericordiae*. . . Omnibus *misericordiae* sinum aperit. . .', *ibid.*, 2; 263, 3ff.

part of the roman toga. It could be used as a pocket, a purse, a hiding place, or a haven.[68] Livy tells of a roman general who would close the fold of his toga if offering to make peace and open it to declare war.[69] 'To have', or 'to receive', someone 'into the fold' (of the toga) meant to make him a trusted friend, a member of the household, to take him under your protection.[70] In the Gospel, *sinus Abrahae* meant being with God.[71] The sculptors of the Middle Ages liked to represent the bosom of Abraham as a huge fold in his mantle held open so souls could come and find their eternal reward. The iconographical theme of the Virgin and her mantle expresses a similar idea: when she spreads her cloak over Christians, our Lady takes them under her protection.[72] So she is truly queen and mother of mercy, whose role is to reconcile and then protect those whom she has brought back into God's favor.

COMMEND US: the words 'commend' and 'recommend' translate the medieval latin word *recommendare*, derived from the classical latin *commendare*, another juridical term from ancient Rome. It comes from *mandare* and means to commit a person or thing, a cause, to someone. The **act** of commending meant entrusting something to another person, often for the purpose of bringing about a happy end. The dying in their wills commended their children to the care of others, or one commended oneself to a 'patron' and thus became his 'client'.[73] In medieval times, 'to commend' meant to place something or someone under the protection of a feudal lord, to entrust it to him. A series of

---

[68]Cf. Stephanus, IV:247–248.

[69]Cf. Stephanus, IV:247–248.

[70]Cf. Forcellini, IV:143.

[71]Lk 16:23.

[72]Cf. P. Perdrizet, *La Vierge de miséricorde. Etude d'un thème iconographique* (Paris, 1908) 1–27, puts the theme of the 'Vierge au manteau' in relation with the advocate title given to Mary by Saint Bernard.

[73]Cf. Stephanus, IV:588–589.

derivative words—*commendatio, commendator, commenda-trix, commendatorius, commendabilis*—express various aspects of the notion of commending.[74]

In the Middle Ages, commend and recommend carried very specific meanings in feudal terminology.[75] They implied protection, expressed in such words as tuition (*tuitio*) and tutelage (*tutela*), even calling up the notion of vassalage. There was no servility in this vassalage, but a promise of faithful service in exchange for protection. The vassal gave himself 'into the hands' of his lord, an act expressed by the ritual gesture of having the vassal kneel and place his joined hands between those of the count or lord to whom he commended himself and promised allegiance, and who in this way acquired the right to command him. This right varied considerably and entailed different legal results. But there was always a real taking-in-charge, a *fideicommis*, or trusteeship, of the person or things which had been commended. To commend oneself meant to seek protection; to commend someone else to another person meant to ask some favor and effective help on his behalf. It meant considerably more than what we imply in using it in a formula like 'letters of recommendation'. In medieval times it implied a formal and reciprocal commitment from which both parties acquired some benefit.

This is the sort of pact Bernard is begging Mary to make between us and her Son: God, in Christ, has made a treaty of friendship (*foedus amicitiarum*[76]) with humanity. Now Jesus is bound to honor his Mother.[77] So she can work things in such a way that he keeps us under his protective tutelage, provided we serve him with loyalty and faithfully.

---

[74]*Thesaurus linguae latinae*, III (Leipzig, 1906–1912) col. 1836, 1854.

[75]*Thesaurus linguae latinae*, III (Leipzig, 1906–1912) col. 1836, 1854.

[76]'. . . ut dando et accipiendo felici *amicitiarum foedere* copulentur humana divinis. . .', Asspt I.2; 229, 17–18.

[77]'Dei Filius *honorare* Matrem', *ibid.*, 24.

REPRESENT US: the classical latin word *repraesentare* originally meant to render someone or something present; to show it as if really present; to place it before someone's eyes. It might simply be a matter of summoning up an image or a memory, but it could also imply a more real presence. Paying a debt or discharging a bequest meant representing the sum or thing owed, that is, making it present again before the legal owner. And furthermore, the re-presentation was effected immediately, without delay, on the exact day and at the precise moment agreed upon.[78]

In the Middle Ages, the word representation still carried the force of its primitive meaning; it had not yet been watered down as it has today when a representative is simply a delegate. Like *praesentare*, to which it was often equated, *repraesentare* signified that something or someone was actually there, being offered, made present. The expression 'to represent in judgement' means to present oneself personally before the judge.[79] In liturgical and theological language 'to represent' a mystery means to render it present in the Church and in individual Christians by grace; this implies on God's side the 'communication' of himself, and on the side of the believer, 'imitation' by which he becomes 'conformed' to the reality received.[80]

In his third sermon for the Purification, Saint Bernard, in speaking of the offering Mary had come to make of her Son in the Temple, addressed her with these words: 'Offer your Son, holy Virgin, and re-present (*repraesenta*) to the Lord the blessed fruit of your womb. Offer him for the reconciliation (*ad reconciliationem*) of us all, a holy sacrifice, acceptable to God. God the Father will wholly accept this

---

[78]Stephanus, IV:87–88.

[79]Du Cange, VII:134–135; Niermeyer 10, 910.

[80]In 'Christusnachfolge und Sakrament in der Theologie des heiligen Bernhards', in *Archiv für Liturgiewissenschaft*, VII, 1 (1963), I have quoted texts.

new offering (*oblationem novam*)'.[81] These words could scarcely have been used with great realism. Mary had received Jesus within herself; she gave him back to God as a present—we could almost say she 'represented her Son to God, and by this act, she contributes to our reconciliation.

If we ask our Lady 'to represent us to her Son', we are begging her to lead us into his presence, to unite us to him in a real and intimate way. Then, as is said further on in the prayer where this phrase occurs, we shall share 'in the same grace, the same privilege, and the same mercy which Mary received, that is to say, the presence of God, and in the world to come we shall participate in the glory and the blessedness of her Son.

CONCLUSION
*A Consistent Theology.*

In the marian texts we have just examined, Bernard consistently used a set of words with a stronger and better defined meaning in medieval law and feudality than the same words or their derivatives to convey to moderns, who might choose other terms to express similar things today. Yet, when we stop to think, when we weigh our words, we should hear their original legal or political overtones reverberating from their feudal context. In this way we shall give them the meaning and the force they had for Bernard and his first readers. Studies of his language of liturgy, mysteries and sacraments have already demonstrated that his terminology expressed more 'realism' than we had realized.[82] The same is true of his marian teaching.

---

[81]'Offer filium, Virgo sacrata, et benedictum fructum ventris tui Domino *repraesenta*. Offer ad nostram omnium *reconciliationem* hostiam sanctam, Deo placentem. Omnino acceptabit Deus Pater oblationem novam . . .', Pur III.2; IV:342, 15–17.

[82] See, *Christusnachfolge und Sakrament.*

When he calls Mary 'Queen of the world', he is thinking of the part she played in the universal salvation of the human race (*ad salutem universitatis*).[83] She performs a real mediation, and this role of mediatrix is rightfully hers for two reasons: in the first place because she is the queen-mother: 'The fruit of your womb is certainly yours in a unique and special way: but, by your mediation he comes to the minds of all persons';[84] secondly, the Virgin continues to be His mother, and consequently she is also our mother when she pleads for us with her Son. In one of his sermons Saint Bernard tells the christian soul: 'On account of the honor due her, she has been heard in your cause, which is that of the whole human race'.[85] 'Cause' here means a legal case, a judicial action in which Mary is the advocate.[86] In another sermon Bernard insists on the universally effective nature of her intervention. 'She has achieved the reparation of the whole world, she has implored salvation for all. For she was solicitous (*sollicita*) of the whole human race'.[87] The word *sollicitus* is both biblical and juridical. Saint Luke had Jesus rebuke Martha: 'You are anxious (*sollicita*) and troubled about many things'.[88] Saint Paul applied it to married men.[89] It suggests disquietude or anxiety. But *sollicitus* can also denote interest in a legal case. In English, to be solicitous means, not only to be anxious, but also deeply concerned, caring, attentive.[90] In

---

[83]Nat BVM 5; V:278, 8.

[84]'Singulariter quidem fructus ventris tui est; sed ad omnium quidem mentes, te *mediante*, pervenit', Ann III.8; 40, 7–8.

[85]'Exaudita est pro reverentia sua in *causa* tua et totius generis humani', V Nat III.10; IV:219, 20–21.

[86]Cf. Niermeyer 2 (1965) 159.

[87]'Haec est enim quae totius mundi *reprarationem* obtinuit, salutem omnium impetravit. Constat enim pro universo genere humano fuisse *sollicitam*', Asspt IV.8; V:249, 21–23.

[88]Lk 10:41.

[89]1 Cor 7:32.

[90]Stephanus IV: 260.

the Middle Ages a solicitor was an agent of the law formally admitted to plead certain cases in a court of justice.[91] When Bernard describes our Lady as *sollicita* for the whole human race, the context seems to suggest that he had in mind the legal sense of the word. Mary takes our cause in hand because she is, in a very real way, our advocate and our queen.

Two observations result from the text analyzed here and the parallels which have been mentioned. In the first place, although Bernard expressed no opinion on the juridical standing of women in society, he did in connection with Mary, marvelously and very specifically transposing the rights of a great lady to the plane of the mystery of salvation. In the second place, this Lady is not only a queen, the spouse of a sovereign, she is also a mother. The theme of the queen-spouse who shares in the king's power (*consors regni*) was frequently used even before Saint Bernard's day; we find it for example, in Rupert of Deutz,[92] Saint

---

[91]Du Cange, VII:521. In the language of tribunals, the French formerly used 'solliciteur' as today the English use 'solicitor' when speaking of certain lawyers. See, for example, E. Littré, *Dictionnaire de la langue française* (Paris, 1871) IV:1971, and H.C. Wyld, *The Universal Dictionary of the English Language* (London, 1934) 1149. Is it necessary to point out that we must be careful not to force the meaning of the words studied here, taking care not to interpret Bernard's words beyond what he meant. My intention has merely been to point out one aspect of his vocabulary. In the case just studied, the isolated words might possibly be devoid of any juridical meaning, but taken together they bring up a question which cannot be left aside. The study of other texts shows that Bernard was equally exact and constant in the use of certain pauline words, as well as of words found in biblical bridal songs, as I have attempted to recall in the article 'La Bible dans les homélies de saint Bernard sur *Missus est*', III: Vocabulaire biblique', in *Studi medievali* 5 (1964) 628–636.

[92]Texts are quoted by M. Bernards, 'Die Frau in der Welt und die Kirche während des 12. Jahrhunderts', in *Sacris erudiri* 20 (1971) 40–48: 'Das Bild der Fürstin'; and in H. Barré, 'La royauté de Marie pendant le XIIe siècle en Occident', in *Maria et Ecclesia. Acta Congressus Mariologici-Mariani in Civitate Lourdes anno 1958 celebrati*, 16 vol. (Rome: Academia Mariana Internationalis, 1959) V:93–111. (This work will henceforth be quoted as *Maria et Ecclesia*). There, in connection with Bernard, we find the terms *imperatrix*, *regina*, *potentia* applied to Mary as queen or mother, but not as queen-mother.

Anselm, Hugh of Saint Victor, and Hildebert of Lavardin.[93] We find it once in Saint Bernard's works, but applied to Charity in relationship to God, in a debate going on between Himself and his own perfections. Bernard wrote to queens and princesses: he never applies to Mary the idea he had of their power, which was, in fact, very limited, except in instances of regency or of a queen with a strong personality exercising personal influence over the king. The image of the queen-mother is more unusual, and also more original and expressive. It too suggests personal influence, but respects the unique transcendence of the person in power. The queen-mother does not wield this power herself; she merely intervenes with the one who possesses it. From a doctrinal point of view this is more exact. It is also more in keeping with Bernard's greater insistence on Mary's motherhood than on her virginity. Virginity is a privilege linked to the part she has in the work of salvation, but she plays this role as a mother. All this argues a very consistent theology.

Finally, on this matter as on every other, Bernard was consistent both with the patterns of thought of his day and the social circles to which he belonged, and also with biblical tradition. Several studies have been done on the royal state of Mary in biblical,[94] patristic,[95] medieval,[96] and

---

[93]'Conversus ad consortem regni Caritatem . . .', Par I.7; VI 2:266, 1.

[94]H. Cazelles, 'Genèse III, 15. Exégèse contemporaine' , in *Études mariales*, IV (1956) 91–99; C. Bleeker, 'The Position of the Queen in Ancient Egypt', in *La Regalità sacra*, VIII Congresso Internazionale di Storia delle Religioni (Rome, 1955) 227–228; M. Peinador, 'Fundamentos escrituristicos de la Realeza de Maria', in *Estudios Marianos* 7 (1956) 27–48.

[95]M. Donnelly, 'The Queenship of Mary during the Patristic Period', in *Marian Studies* 4 (1953) 82–108.

[96]H. Barré, 'La royauté de Marie pendant les neuf premiers siècles', in *Recherches de sciences religieuses* 29 (1939) 129–162, 303–334; V. Hill, 'Our Lady's Queenship in the Middle Ages and Modern Times', in *Marian Studies* 4 (1953) 134–169.

liturgical[97] literature, as well as from the point of view of systematic theology.[98] Two of these studies have dealt with the theme of the queen-mother in Scripture.[99] According to the most recent and better documents of them, 'believers in the time [of Christ] were well aware from the Old Testament that the king's mother was not, as she is today, a widow set more or less to the side. On the contrary she held a privileged position, she was associated with the government of her son'.[100] Cazelles demonstrates this first of all by witnesses from middle-eastern civilizations of the second millennium before Christ, where the queen was 'more honored as mother than as spouse of the king'[101] and where she played a political role.[102] She was associated with the government of her son.[103] The same situation crops up in several biblical texts: Genesis, Kings, the prophets and, in particular, a passage of Isaiah (7:14) which is evoked in the account of the Annunciation. 'Associated with her Son at birth, his mother remained so all the while the mystery of the Word was being revealed to us'.[104] Mary is the associate of her divine Son in his earthly birth, in his royal governance, and in his glory.[105] We find in Saint Bernard the same right note in this conciliation of the

---

[97]G. Frénaud, 'La royauté de Marie dans la liturgie' in *Maria et Ecclesia* 5:57–92.

[98]T. Bartolomee, 'Fondamenti della regalità di Maria' in *Ephemerides Mariologicae* 15 (1965) 49–82; summary in G. Kirwin, *The Nature of the Queenship of Mary* (Washington D.C., 1973) 379.

[99]U. Donner, 'Art und Herkunft des Amtes der Königsmutter im Alten Testament', in *Festschrift J. Friedrich* (Heidelberg, 1959) 101–145; H. Cazelles, 'La Mère du Roi-Messie dans l'Ancien Testament' in *Maria et Ecclesia* 5 39–56.

[100]H. Cazelles, *La Mère du Roi-Messie*, p. 49.

[101]*Ibid.*, p. 41.

[102]*Ibid.*, p. 47.

[103]*Ibid.*, p. 48.

[104]*Ibid.*, p. 55.

[105]*Ibid.*, p. 56.

transcendant superiority of Jesus united to the Word, and in the role Mary played as his mother.

## 4. *God in the Feminine.*

Does femininity have some part in the representation Bernard made of God, in the language he used to speak of him? Two things lead us to pose this question.

First of all, a lot is being said today about everything in the christian tradition, and pre-christian traditions, concerning the feminine in general and its relationship with God in particular. Some studies deal with the Bible as a whole,[106] some with either the Old or the New Testament by itself.[107] The importance of feminine images are more and more being recognized. In the Old Testament the prevailing image is the maternal womb, the 'symbol of divine compassion'.[108] Behind this metaphor and the terms which translate it lies a root which in Hebrew means the gratuitous kindness which creates, gratifies, and forgives, as a mother does, and which corresponds to the word 'mercy', *misericordia*, in Latin. Correlatively, the people which constitutes the object of this maternal love is portrayed as a daughter, a fiancée or a bride. None of all this excludes the idea of fatherly love. At least other feminine comparisons are frequently associated with the primitive term and its derivatives. They give greater wealth of meaning to the notion of a God whose love communicates life and then maintains it by nurturing it, restores life when necessary, bestows fecundity, and brings consolation and comfort. Since Bernard's language is thoroughly biblical,

---

[106]For example, Leonard Swidler, *Biblical Affirmations of Women* (Philadelphia, 1979).

[107]R. Hamilton-Kelly, 'God the Father in the Bible and in the Experience of Jesus: The State of the Question' in Metz-Schillebeecks, *God as Father?* = *Concilium* 143 (1981) 95–102.

[108]I shall summarize here the article by P. Trible, 'God, (Nature of), in the OT', in *The Interpreter's Dictionary of the Bible. Supplementary Volume* (Abingdon-Nashville, 1976) 368–369.

we may rightly wonder how much of all this passes into his writings. The question is still more legitimate in that the latin patristic and medieval traditions, both before Saint Bernard and during his century and afterwards, inherited all these images and used them in an authentic and very lofty spiritual theology.[109]

Furthermore, more than one person has attempted to apply to Saint Bernard's texts the theories of the philosopher Carl Gustav Jung. Several unpublished essays have been written on this subject. Now, one of the basic jungian ideas is the complementarity of the masculine and the feminine. The latter evokes the sphere of the unconscious which must be integrated with the conscious, the masculine. There is no need here to expound on these ideas, or on the applications which could be made to Saint Bernard. That field of research has yet to be methodically explored. Saint Bernard has been likened to a mother to his monks, and some of his own phrases concur with this manner of speaking, which is William of Saint Thierry's.[110] According to Jung, this feminine element, like the masculine, has two aspects, one positive and one negative. To be honest, the investigation would have to be very complex and carefully nuanced. It could only be correctly carried out by someone, or by several researchers, knowledgable in history, philosophy, twelfth-century theology, and especially in Saint Bernard, and Jung's teaching.

Here I shall do no more than present a few of the many possible texts, and my reading will be, so to speak, naive, devoid of technicalities. But at least it should help to show the grounds for the twin question which has been asked in the light of contemporary theology and psychology. The delicate thing about interpreting and translating texts of

---

[109]In the Preface to *Julian of Norwich. Showings* (New York, 1978) 8–14, I have given fuller examples.

[110]Texts are indicated in A. Dimier, *Saint Bernard pêcheur de Dieu* (Paris, 1953) 143–153.

Saint Bernard is that they are all in Latin. Words do not have the grammatical gender they had in their original biblical tongues, or have in modern non-romance languages. But since Latin is the language Bernard used, it is the one which interests us here: it conveys his mind-sets. Right away we notice that nearly all abstract words applied to the mystery of God—those ending most often in *-ia, -as* or *-do* (for example, *sapientia, caritas, fortitudo*)— are feminine in gender.

One of the ways of tackling these texts and putting them into some sort of order is by examining them from the point of view of the unfolding history of salvation, starting with the creation of man. The first of the sermons for the Annunciation took as its theme Psalm 84, verse 10: 'That glory might dwell in our land, mercy and faithfulness will meet; righteousness and justice will kiss each other'. This immediately presents us with four realities which come into play in the working-out of God's plan. They were behind a theme widely illustrated in the Middle Ages in preaching, liturgical drama, and iconography: the debate or conflict among the 'daughters of God'. The text of this first sermon for the Annunciation exists in two drafts, one of which is specifically presented in the form of a debate. According to the manuscript tradition, it is to this first, spontaneous draft that Saint Bernard afterwards, as he prepared it for publication gave a literary form more befitting a proper sermon.[111] But his train of thought is identical in the two drafts.

God's intention is given at the beginning: he wants to send down to humankind his own Wisdom, his Son, so that his own glory might dwell in our land. To this end he prepares certain creatures to receive his Wisdom, his eternal Son, the Incarnate Word. He therefore confers on humankind four major gifts: the capacity for mercy, faith-

---

[111] See the two drafts in SBOp. V:17–29; *PL* 18:385–390 gives the second draft.

fulness, righteousness, and peace. Bernard explains each in turn (Ann I.6). Through sin, man lost these gifts by which he was like unto God. He retained, however, the deep image (7). After the sin of Adam and Eve, these four virtues, having returned to God, quarrel in his presence, or more precisely, in him. Bernard paints for us a family scene in which all the actors are women (9). God speaks to each as to 'sisters' (10,11). At the end, it is Mercy, in other words Charity, who wins (12–13). The Incarnation is decided. The sisters are reconciled, and Justice and Peace, in particular, conclude a treatise of unbreakable friendship. This is the conclusion: 'Whoever receives the testimony of Justice will be greeted by Peace with a smiling face and gentle embrace, finding in her rest and sleep' (14). In this long passage all the terms used to describe the action within God are feminine.

In his treatise *On Grace and Free Choice*, Bernard also speaks of the restoration of God's image in man. He compares 'the incarnate Wisdom of God' to the woman in the Gospel who lights her lamp, sweeps her house—that is to say, cleans it out, throwing out all vices—, and finds the lost coin, that is to say, her own image; and then makes it once again like himself. In this marvelous page, God is thus searching for himself, his Wisdom is in quest of self. There then follows a very beautiful passage on the Wisdom which is God himself, the source of all freedom (32–34).

The theme of liberation, of freedom, comes up again, amplified, in a long parable[112]: Sinful man is represented as the son of a powerful king. Still a young man, he has broken away from his tutors and become an abandoned child. This time Bernard uses the Gospel parable of the prodigal son. But the father shows the feelings of a mother: as is said in Isaiah (49:15), can he, or rather can she, 'forget the son of her womb?' Not only does he not forget, but he shows mercy and compassion. He sends out to the son

---

[112] Par I; VI/2: 261–267.

symbols of himself, and nearly all of them have, in Latin, a feminine name. Hope, in particular, 'approaches the lost son with gentleness', consoles him, and wipes his eyes and his face. When he asks her how she could have come to him in his despair, she replies 'I am Hope, sent by God to help you until I can bring you into your father's house, into the room of her who begot you'. The son replies 'Oh, the gentle comfort of my sorrows, the sweet consolation of the wretched! So you are one, and not the least, of those, who are in attendance in the king's chamber!' Hope then reassures him, putting under his feet the soft carpet of devotion. Prudence arrives, with her friend Temperance, and, most important, Wisdom. She it is who greets the prodigal son on his return, welcoming him like a mother, carrying him in her arms, bringing him into her own home, and laying him down to rest on a bed which echoes from the Song of Songs. But the child is kidnapped, and this brings a new episode into the drama. Wisdom calls upon prayer and faith. Charity has the last word, for she shares the power of the king. And at once this queen of heaven, accompanied with the whole heavenly court sets out. She takes back the child of God. Queen Charity carries the child up to heaven and offers him to God the Father, who orders a homecoming feast. Through all of this, God's sentiments are those of a woman, of a mother, at least as much as they are those of a man, and are in keeping with symbols taken from the Old Testament.

The same is true in Parable Two, which in a succession of scenes represents the same story of salvation, by using different stories. Here again Justice delegates to God's service Prayer, who, led once again into his chamber, talks to him as Esther did to King Ahasuerus. Moved to tears, he decides to send Charity to man, lost by sin. And Charity, already familiar with him, volunteers. She takes Peace, Patience, Kindness, Goodness, and Gentleness to accompany her. Like Esther or Judith, she passes through all the ramparts, the doors, the guards. In the camp of Israel they ask who she is. Charity has all doors opened to her and, with her army, carries off the final victory (Par II; VI/2: 267–273). In all this is brought into play a whole register of images we did not find in the preceding parable. Yet common to both are the feminine images and events drawn from the Old Testament.

In Parable Four, the Church is a bride, and God united himself to her, first creating her in his own image, and then in freeing her from the captivity of sin. Again the whole story is told by means of the images of Old Testament women to whom God had shown his mercy (SBOp VI/2: 277–281). In the next parable, God intervenes by the mediation of Charity and her friend Piety, the 'royal daughters'. Charity is a Lady. Here again, they play roles similar to those of the Old Testament heroines who helped save the People of God (Par V; VI/2:282–285).

Finally, one of Bernard's favorite themes is the Wisdom of God which, as the Book of Proverbs says, has built herself a house (9:1) in Mary and in each Christian. With herself, this heavenly Wisdom introduces into the dwelling she has built Justice, Prudence, Temperance, and Fortitude (Div 52: VI/1:274–277), all the many daughters of God who are sisters to each other, as Bernard had already said in other texts.

We have not been able to do more than quote a few of the examples of feminine qualities attributed to God. Bernard's whole work would require careful examination from this point of view. Many other cases could be found. But for the time being we need only observe one fact: according to Bernard, feminine metaphors can be applied to God just as legitimately as masculine ones. And this fact is very simply explained by the influence the language of the Bible had on his thought.

# CHAPTER VI

# MYTHS ABOUT SAINT BERNARD

YTHS ALLEGING Bernard's antifeminism are long-
lived and die hard, like those about the exaggerated place he is supposed to have given the
Virgin Mary in his works. To be historically objective we
must examine these texts very carefully and evaluate their
true worth.

Three of these myths occur in a text which, according to
its author himself, was written without Bernard's knowledge —*nec ipso nesciente*— and consequently, without his
having been consulted. Furthermore, as has been shown,
this text tells us more about the author's problems than
about Bernard's. The text in question is Book I of the *Vita
prima*, which William of Saint Thierry had completed before his own death in 1148, that is to say, five years before
Bernard's death.[1] William did not know Bernard during
the period of his life he narrates there. Once he had become
a Cistercian at Signy, it did not enter his mind to interview
Bernard's brothers at Clairvaux or any other witness who
could have given him accurate information. He used notes
or 'Fragments' put together with an eye on a *Life* of Saint
Bernard, by Geoffrey of Auxerre, who met Bernard for the

---

[1]Text in PL 185: 225–268.

first time in 1140.[2] Geoffrey's idea was not so much to write an historical biography as to prepare a background document for his eventual canonization. William had the same intention and adopted the same literary genre, adding three edifying stories about Bernard's youth to the events related by Geoffrey.[3] We must examine these texts in turn.

## 1. Hagiographical Themes.

Some writers have taken to explaining the misogyny attributed to Saint Bernard—and everything else in his behavior and writings—by a state of habitual repression in which he is supposed to have lived throughout his life from adolescence onward. What this thesis relies on—for thesis it is—is no more than an hagiographical commonplace proposed as an historical event. And, after all, such an event is not unlikely. But if it did happen, we must be careful to verify its accuracy and meaning. According to this story, Bernard was tempted physically and threw himself into an icy pond; as a result he decided to live in celibacy. But this would not have prevented what is bred in the bones from coming out in the flesh, as an old expression has it.[4] In fact, according to the earliest and least 'interpreted' witness, that is to say, Geoffrey of Auxerre's text, Bernard had already decided to 'convert' to the monastic life and had even begun to convert his brothers when this incident is supposed to have occurred. In middle eastern deserts, where water was rare, to plunge into a pond would have been much more an occasion of pleasure.

---

[2]Text edited by R. Lechat, 'Les Fragmenta de Vita et Miraculis sancti Bernardi par Geoffroy d'Auxerre', in *Analecta Bollandiana*, 50 (1932) 83–122.

[3]On the nature of this Book I, see *Nouveau visage*, 15–34.

[4] On this charge and on the consequences which certain people have thought possible to draw from this passage of the *Vita prima*, I.6–7; *PL* 185: 230, a bibliography is found in 'Agressivité et répression chez Bernard de Clairvaux', in *Revue d'histoire de la spiritualité* 52 (1976) 156–157.

This is probably one of the reasons why there was traditionally a certain caution against baths.[5] Other examples
could be added to those collected by Louis Gougaud, and
also certain variations of the story. Saint Benedict, for
example, instead of jumping into Lake Subiaco, rolled
himself in thorns, or so we are told by Saint Gregory the
Great in a delightful fable. Pierre Courcelle concludes his
study with these words: 'As for myself, I have trouble
accepting the episode as historical.'[6] Other saints are supposed to have thrown themselves into fire or applied fiery
brands to themselves.[7] The imagination, or rather the
memory, of hagiographers could choose from among several variations.[8]

Two other tests of Bernard's virtue, according to William's legend, did not require a great deal of imagination
on his part, nor even an effort of memory, for they are to be
found in many a legend. The first, not at all improbable,
and paralleled by many examples in every era without
exception, consists in having a girl enter Bernard's room at

---

[5]See A. de Vogüé, *La Règle de S.Benoît* VI, Sources chrétiennes, 186
(Paris, 1971) 1100–1103, with bibliography [ET *The Rule of St Benedict. A
Doctrinal and Spiritual Commentary*, CS54 (1983)] Behind this reserve also
lay precautions against seeing the naked body; a strange exception is
that of Simeon the New Theologian, *Hymn 15*, 140–2–39, edd. J. Koder &
J. Paramelle, *Sources chrétiennes*, 156 (Paris, 1969) 289–297; see *ibid.*,
71–72. On this case and on jumping naked into thorns or snow, see texts
and evaluations in the article '*Nudità*' in the *Dizionario degli Istituti di
Perfezione* VI (Rome, 1980) 474–475.

[6]P. Courcelle, 'Saint Benoît, le merle et le buisson d'épines' in *Journal
des savants* (1967) 161. M. Doucet, 'La tentation de saint Benoît: relation
ou création par saint Grégoire le Grand?', *Collectanea Cisterciensia* 37
(1975) 63–71, comes to the same conclusion.

[7]This is what is related about Saint William Firmat, *AA SS* Apr. III
(1675) 335.

[8]Saint Louis, during the nights of voluntary continency he spent with
his wife, simply walked up and down the room, according to E.R.
Labande, 'Quelques traits du caractère du roi Saint Louis', *Revue d'histoire de la spiritualité* 50 (1974) 143.

night.[9] The story resembles in many points one which we find, for example, in the life of Saint Thomas Aquinas.[10] In these cases, details vary according to circumstances, but they all have two elements in common: the solicitation; and the fruit of temptation overcome, that is, the gift of continence. The saint in question decides to preserve his virginity and receives grace, which in no way means that he will be insensitive ever afterwards.

A third hagiographical theme served to illustrate not only the saint's victory over himself, but also the masterly strength of his virtue. That a chaste person should be solicited by someone unchaste is a constant in the Old Testament from Joseph onward. We come across it too in the lives of virtuous people in paganism.[11] But christian legends often add the conversion of the temptress. We find this, for example, in the legend of martyrs, like martyrs of the Thebaide,[12] or of Saint Christopher,[13] or again, Saint Ephrem,[14] and Saint Martinian.[15] In the legend William of

---

[9] 'In lectum dormientis infecta est puella nuda... Misera vero illa aliquandiu iacuit sustinens et exspectans, deinde palpans et stimulans', *Vita prima*, I.7; *PL* 185:230.

[10]'Miserunt ad ipsum solum existentem in camera... puellam pulcherrimam... quae ipsum aspectu, tactu, ludis, et quibus posset aliis modis alliceret ad peccandum', Willian of Tocco, *Vita sancti Thomae Aquinatis*, AA SS. Boll., *Mart. I*; 659–660. W.A. Wallace and J.A. Weisheipel, 'Thomas Aquinas, St.', in *The New Catholic Encyclopedia* (New York, 1967) XIV: col. 103, judged this story to be a legend with very little historical truth, and H. Vicaire, 'L'homme que fut saint Thomas', in N.A. Layten, ed., *L'anthropologie de saint Thomas* (Fribourg, 1974) 29, n.6, writing of the 'artifice de la courtisane', says that it is not new, and refers to an earlier story.

[11] For example, in *Philostratus, The Life of Appolonius of Tyana* (Cambridge, Mass.–London, 1969) I: 28–30; but there the incident is in a greek context: solicitation to homosexuality.

[12]*AA SS* Iul. VI (1729) 544.

[13]*Ibid.*, 147, n. 5–6.

[14]*Vita sancti Ephraem*, 5; *PL* 73:322.

[15]See Baudot-Chaussin, *Vie des saints et des bienheureux* II (Paris, 1936) 305–307.

Saint-Thierry composed, we are not told whether the lady of the castle, Bernard's hostess and temptress, mended her ways. But the adventure is enlivened by the insertion of a few details which relieve the monotony an all too familiar theme could well have caused. Bernard is supposed to have called out three times 'Stop thief!', because the woman was trying to rob him of his virtue. If this is historically true, the way Bernard and his companions joked about it the next day certainly gives the impression of balance and freedom, rather than gloomy repression.[16]

A special question comes to mind in connection with this third temptation because there was a certain medieval practice which makes it not unlikely. There existed in those days a custom by which a knight staying at a castle was offered the host's daughter, or even his wife, for the night. If we are to believe some literary sources after Bernard's time—especially after the days of his youth— the laws of hospitality required a series of courtesies: the guest was first welcomed and his host expressed joy and honor at receiving him; he was relieved of his heavy armor and his horse was taken to the stables to be cared for; he was invited to take a meal and someone sat with him while he ate, conversing with him and showing him every form of consideration. Then one or more of the women of the household kissed his face and his hands. All these signs of kindly welcome were generally reserved for members of the family and not accorded to strangers.[17] Romance writers and authors of *fabliaux* enliven their accounts with titillating details about the way the visitor was 'served': the women put their arms round him, kissed, hugged, mas-

---

[16]See Baudot-Chaussin, *Vie des saints et des bienheureux* II (Paris, 1936) 305–307.

[17]On all these points, texts are cited and commented on by H. Oschinsky, *Der Ritter unterwegs die Pflege Gastfreundschaft im Alten Frankreich* (Halle, 1900) 46–75.

saged and caressed him until he fell asleep.[18] The noble-woman was thus reduced to being nothing more than an instrument of the knight's pleasure and rest. We even read that he sometimes resisted such overtures and pushed the woman away.

The lady of the castle is supposed to have solicited Bernard one night when, he, along with his brothers, was her husband's guest. If this custom really existed when Bernard was a young man, it would explain the fact that he joked about it the next day with his group of companions, for everyone would have known that such a thing could happen.[19] Furthermore, it seems curious that the lady should have tried to seduce Bernard, and not one of the other young men of the group. But this favoritism, if we may call it that, is quite easily explained if the author of the story wanted to exalt his hero and his virtues above all the others, which is the usual thing in saints' lives.

In fact, everything leads us to think that the theme here is not the knight's comfort but simply a hagiographical commonplace. None of the many documents generally cited in connection with this supposed custom has an historical nature. They are nothing but short stories and *fabliaux* written by men trying to divert their audience or readers by inserting spicy tid-bits. Had there been any frequent or general moral deviation, it would very probably have been denounced by moralists like Bernard of Worms who seems to have foreseen every possible case. And furthermore, the care the nobility took to assure pure blood in their offspring and the continuation of their lineage makes it hardly probable that a man would risk either his wife or his daughter having a child by a transient knight. It is nevertheless possible that such a practice was

---

[18]What is said there, pp. 74–75, about the sense of the french word 'tastonner' could shed light on the meaning of the word *pertractare* used by William of Saint Thierry in the passage of the *Vita prima Bernardi* referred to in the following note.

[19] *Vita prima*, I.7; PL 185: 230–231.

kept up in some places to attract to the castle a noble with whom the family was anxious to have marriage ties.

Did William of Saint-Thierry know about this custom? We can do no more than conjecture on this point. But he certainly knew about this sort of temptation as it is related by biblical, monastic, and hagiographical tradition. To the examples given elsewhere,[20] more could be added. And it is quite understandable that in Saint Bernard's own century, the *Life of Christine of Markyate*,[21] and in the following century, the *Life of Blessed Gerald of Sales*,[22] should contain similar stories.[23] But the *First Life* of Saint Bernard offers no historical evidence for any aggression or solicitation he underwent in his youth. We can however evaluate the harm done to his reputation by the legends his admirer, William of Saint Thierry, included. They were later taken as historical truth by people who then drew quite unjustified conclusions about Bernard's attitude towards women.

## 2. *The Bag of Dung.*

Among other things, Bernard is accused of having considered woman a bag of manure.[24] Neither the words nor the idea they suggest are to be found in his writings. One wonders which text inspired such a reproach. Probably a line written by William of Saint Thierry about the visit of

---

[20]*Nouveau visage . . .* , 160.

[21]C.H. Talbot, *The Life of Christina of Markyate. A Twelfth Century Recluse* (Oxford, 1959).

[22]After M.O. Lenglet, 'La biographie du bienheureux Géraud de Sales ( + 1120)', in *Cîteaux* 27 (1976) 27, citing a text written towards the end of the thirteenth century.

[23]The solicitation could be intended to see whether in the event of a marital lawsuit, the partner was impotent, as in the case related by J.A. Brundage, 'Matrimonial Politics in Thirteenth Century Aragon: Moncada v. Urgel', in *The Journal of Ecclesiastical History* 3 (1980) 280.

[24]For example, M. Payen, 'Discussion', in *Cahiers de civilisation médiévale* 20 (1977) 128.

Humbeline, 'married in the world and given to things of the world'. She is supposed to have come to see her brother Bernard when he was a young abbot at Clairvaux, as well as her other brothers who had followed him to the monastery.[25] She is supposed to have come with an elegant retinue and Bernard, wrote William, 'hating and loathing her as if she were a snare of the devil set on luring souls, refused to go out to see her'. She complained. But Andrew, one of her brothers and Bernard's, being the doorkeeper 'seems to have rebuked her with being a parcel of dung, because of her elegant clothes'.[26] And, so the story relates, she was touched to the quick and decided to change her life.

All this must be written in the conditional for there is nothing to guarantee that it really happened. Everything, in fact, leads us to think it is all pure invention. Notice first that the rebuke is attributed, not to Bernard, but to his brother Andrew. 'Attributed', I say, because we find nothing about this incident in the *Fragments* of Geoffrey of Auxerre which, despite their hagiographical inclinations, might guarantee a certain authenticity. Yet there is no mention of the incident. Moreover, it is well-known that such scenes are part and parcel of the legendary themes from antiquity onwards and are meant to illustrate the fact that monks were to break with their families.[27] The rebuke under discussion cannot be attributed even to Andrew; he is hardly likely to have had any knowledge of such hagiographical texts. But William did, just as he knew about other themes already discussed above. The commonplaces

---

[25]*Vita prima*, I.30; *PL* 185: 244–245. The whole context, which can only be summarized here, is important for the interpretation of this text.

[26]'Cum a fratre suo Andrea, quem ad portam invenerat monasterii, ob vestium apparatum stercus involutum argueretur . . . ', *ibid.*, 244D.

[27]See *Nouveau visage*, p. 19, n. 33, for bibliography on this theme in monastic hagiography.

of the visit and Andrew's rebuke are due entirely to William of Saint Thierry who depended on literary tradition.

Again, this does not concern womankind in general, or each and every woman, but simply the worldly sister of a group of monks she had come to 'seduce'; one more temptation to add to those already facing Saint Bernard. And Humbeline, far from taking umbrage at this reproach as a personal insult, grasped its real meaning. She set about living the austere life of a hermit, to such an extent that her husband, greatly edified by his wife's conduct, set her free from their marriage bonds so she might become a nun. It is within this context, with all it includes of hagiographical invention and literary exaggeration, that we must read the words about elegant clothes wrapping up muck. When we read the speeches ascribed to a hero of the arthurian cycle or a courtly romance, do we naively believe that King Arthur or any other historical person really uttered these words? Let us adopt the same attitude with regard to words William put into the mouth of Saint Bernard's brother.

But where did William get this commonplace? The image is not biblical. We can find it in pre-christian, non-western civilizations, in Jainism, for example. Among certain peoples, the Aztecs and others, filth and ordure are associated with the notion of sin. In some tribes of Black Africa, it is supposed to penetrate the body of a woman. To be brief, we already see that excrement symbolizes, among other things, shameful contempt. It is a sort of universal archetype. It is not surprising that it should have surfaced from time to time in the greek and latin literature which influenced the Fathers of the Church and, consequently, the literature of the Middle Ages. It would surely be possible, after careful research, to collate a number of references. We could point to a sentence of Odo, abbot of Cluny in the tenth century, which contains the phrase *stercoris saccum*, bag of dung.[28] This is part of a long tirade warning monks and nuns against the temptations which might arise from elegance in dress and physical attractiveness. 'Ah! if we had the eyes of a Boeotian lynx, we would be able to see what is inside . . . ' Now, this was written about all human beings not specifically and exclusively about women. Sometimes, however, the idea was applied to women, and in similar contexts, that is, in speaking, not of womankind in general, but simply of the danger their visits pose to monks and clerics vowed to celibacy. This is the case in a long poem by Roger of Caen, a monk of Bec who died after 1095. He mentions the peril posed by an elegant 'sinful woman' given to visiting the cells of the cloister.[29] In the hope of discouraging the monks from giving in to temptation, the author describes the inconveniences of living with a woman, even in faithful wedlock. He hastens to add that he in no way wishes to condemn the legitimate union of the marriage bed but merely to stress the fact that such joys are not for men who have chosen to seek perfection in the monastic state.[30]

After William of Saint Thierry's day there were other cases when this theme was used. A pseudo-Augustine at the beginning of the thirteenth century, for example, applied it to everyone, man and woman alike.[31] Alexander Neckham ( + 1227) repeated it with the aim of convincing

---

[28]*Collationes*, II.9; *PL* 133:556.

[29]*Carmen de contemptu mundi*, sometimes called *De monachis* in the manuscripts, *PL* 158:697B. It is perhaps because of this pseudo-Anselm that the same anti-feminism has been attributed to both Saint Anselm and Saint Bernard. On the author, see M. Manitius, *Geschichte der lateinischen Literatur des Mittelalters*, III (1931) col. 851–852.

[30]*Carmen de contemptu mundi*; 698B.

[31]*Soliloquia*, II.2; *PL* 40:866–867. The author is an anonymous writer of the thirteenth century, at least after the Lateran Council of 1198, according to F. Cavallera, art. 'Augustin (saint): Apocryphes', in *Dictionnaire de spiritualité* 1 (1937) col. 1134.

monks to remain in continence.[32] Adam of Perseigne mentioned it in a letter to the Countess of Perche, advising her
to avoid all vain elegance.[33] Then the theme was adopted
by the authors of the *exempla*.[34] The scene imagined by
William of Saint Thierry is sometimes summarized in a few
lines and without the slightest reference to Saint Bernard.[35]
But in Gilbert of Tournai, an allusion to the lynx eyes
inspired by the text of Odo of Cluny is followed by Bernard's name and a formula which has nothing to do with
him, and which, furthermore, applies to both men and
women.[36] And so it was that, from then on, this commonplace was transmitted under Bernard's name, and used by
compilers who read neither Bernard nor William of Saint
Thierry, as is equally true of certain present day authors.

Though not frequent, then, the theme of the bag of dung
is found in medieval literature. Saint Bernard alludes to it
four times. When quoting Galatians 6:8 where Saint Paul
associates the seed of human life with the need to go
through a stage of decay, he compares to filth what the
Apostle called the 'flesh', or 'the body of sin', that is, the
place of concupiscence and the cause of corruption, as
opposed to the soul, that is, the Spirit, cause of eternal life

---

[32]The text is cited and studied by A. Wulff, *Die fraufeindlichen Dichtungen in den romanischen Literaturen des Mittelalters bis zum Ende des XIII.
Jahrhunderts* (Halle, 1914) 28–30.

[33]Letter XV.160, ed. J. Bouvet, *Adam de Perseigne. Lettres*, I, *Sources
chrétiennes* 66 (Paris, 1960) 240. This text was probably written between
1191 and 1202: see *ibid.*, pp. 240–241, n.1 [English translation by Grace
Perigo, *The Letters of Adam of Perseigne*, CF 21 (1976) 196–7].

[34]References in F.C. Tubach, *Index exemplorum. A Handbook of Medieval
Religious Tales* (Helsinki, 1969) p. 51, n.615.

[35]Ed. J. Th. Welter, *La Tabula exemplorum secundum ordinem alphabeti.
Recueil d'exemples compilés en France à la fin du XIIIᵉ siècle* (Paris, 1926) p. 52,
n.187.

[36]'Si habuerimus oculos ut carnis parietem penetrarent, videremus
intestina mulierum plena stercoribus et fecibus . . . Bernardus: Quid est
pulchritudo carnis nisi velamen turpitudinis?', *Ad conjugatos, sermo III*,
cited in *Prediche alle donne, del secolo XIII*, a cura di C. Casagrande (Milan,
1978) p. 95; there is no reference to any source.

(Div 82.2; VI/1:322,15–16). Elsewhere, and in the same sense, Bernard uses the word *sterquilinium* in connection with the wretched body' as contrasted with 'the heart where Christ dwells' (Div 5.4; VI/1:102,12–13). A similar image is discreetly summoned up about this 'body of sin' which, says Bernard, exists in himself and in all of us: until we are united with Christ in his glory, 'we are shut up in the horrible prison of a body stinking of muck (*faeculentum corpus*), we are shackled by sin and death' (Ep 144.1; VII:344, 16–17). In his sermon for the Ascension, we find similar phrases again, but they are applied only to monks who are not yet converted and do not even blush at the fact; they are, as Jeremiah says (3:3), brazen as harlots (Asc 3.5; V:135, 6–7).

Bernard knew about the bag of dung, then. And though he applied it to himself and to his monks, not once did he use it about women. In short, this somewhat vulgar commonplace allows us, by way of contrast, so to speak, to appreciate the soundness of Bernard's teaching on women and the delicacy with which he speaks of them.

## 3. *Bernard and Mills.*

It is likely the end of letter 79 which has given rise to a queer interpretation that a simple reading of the text would have obviated. Under the pretext that harlots, so it seems, congregated near mills in the hope of finding clients 'Saint Bernard, . . . scandalized to hear of the prostitutes' activities, threatened to have the mills closed. If such a thing had occurred . . . the european economy would have grown at a far slower rate'.[37] In this interpretative passage, the author is dealing with the whole of the Middle Ages and the whole of Europe. One wonders in the name of what authority and with what power Bernard could

---

[37] J. Gimpel, *The Medieval Machine. The Industrial Revolution of the Middle Ages* (New York, 1976) 3.

have put into effect a decision of such far-reaching consequences.[38]

What do we really read in Saint Bernard's text? This:

There is still one other piece of business about which I
cannot help telling you what I think—with my usual
impertinence. It concerns that mill which the lay-
brothers in charge allow to be frequented by many
women. If you want my opinion, you should do one
of two things: either forbid women access to this mill,
or entrust it to some outsider, but not to the lay-
brothers; or else give it up altogether (Ep 79.3; VII:212,
10–15).

In the text, as we see, there is no mention of prostitutes, or
of mills in France in general, or of their suppression.[39]
True, the upkeep of mills presented economic problems to
monasteries in the Middle Ages, but Bernard had nothing
to do with the solution of them. In a long study which has
recently been devoted to this source of energy in the
twelfth century, Bernard is never named.[40] Then, and

---

[38]The interpretation goes on to say: 'The effect would have been in
some way comparable to that produced by the 1973 decision of the oil-
producing countries in the Middle East to raise the price of oil and put an
embargo on supplies to certain countries of the Western world. The
economy of the West has been affected by these measures . . .', *ibid.*

[39]Doubtless the connection between mills and prostitutes should not
be exaggerated. For example, a well documented study on the place of
mills in the economy and culture of a specific region of Italy, does not
mention prostitutes: C. Dessain, 'Les moulins à Reggio d'Emilie aux XIIe
et XIIIe siècles', in *Mélanges de l'Ecole Française de Rome, Moyen Age - Temps
modernes* 91/1 (1971) 113–147.

[40]D. Lohrmann, 'Energie probleme im Mittelalter: Zur Verknappung
von Wasserkraft im Holz in Westeuropa bis zum Ende des 12. Jahrhunderts', in *Vierteljahrschrift für Sozial-und Wirtschaftsgeschichte* 66 (1979)
297–316. On Cistercians and mills, see W. Braunfels, *Abendländische
Klosterbaukunst* (Cologne, 1969) 305–310, ET, *Monasteries of Western Europe*
(1972) 94, and W. Schich, 'Die Wirtschafstätigkeit der Zistercienser im
Mittelalter: Handel und Gewerbe', in *Zistercienser. Ordensleben zwischen
Ideal und Wirklichkeit* (Bonn, 1980) 217–220.

later, the cistercian General Chapters more than once had
to draw up statutes about mills.[41] In England and elsewhere, operating mills gave rise to conflicts between monasteries and to clashes of interests with their neighbors.[42]
Bernard did not meddle in these affairs except in the few
lines quoted above.

On the other hand, we find in Bernard's works the
theme of the 'mystic mill', inspired by texts of Holy Scripture, recurring seven times, and closely connected with
other themes: the winds turning the sails and the press it
sets into action. The mill, according to Bernard, in the light
of tradition, 'represents the passion of Christ' and either
'the trial of death, or the suffering which purifies and
refines the soul it crushes, and is so useful for salvation'.[43]
An allegory of this kind implies a very precise knowledge
of what a mill really is. These texts of Bernard were translated very early into French and served to inspire preachers
and sculptors. If he has any place in the history of mills,
it is on account of these sermons and not the last part of
letter 79.

## 4. *Class anti-feminism?*

The author of a recent work on *Town and Life of the Spirit
in the High Middle Ages* strives to apply to the twelfth
century the theories of Frederick Engels and Lenin, both
repeatedly mentioned in the Introduction. He also em-
ploys the theory of Karl Marx, and concludes his work on

---

[41]References in J.M. Canivez, *Statuta Capitulorum Generalium Ordinis
Cisterciensis*, VII (Louvain, 1941) 335, at the word *Molendinum*.

[42]For example, Bennett D. Hill, *English Cistercian Monasteries and their
Patrons in the Twelfth Century* (Urbana-Chicago-London: University of
Illinois Press, 1968) p. 68 and *passim*.

[43]On these texts and their influence, M. Zink, 'Moulin mystique. A
propos d'un chapiteau de Vézelay: figures allégoriques dans la prédi-
cation et dans l'iconographie romane', in *Annales E.E.S.* 31 (1976)
481–489.

the last page with two quotations to prove his own theories. As Werner sees things, the history of this and every other period is one of the struggle between two classes: that of 'feudalism' established in country places, and that of the townspeople, oppressed and alienated and managing to become emancipated. It is in this context that we read the following lines about Bernard:

> Bernard's attitude to the classes comes out in his dealings, in conversation or in writing, with ladies of noble stock and with nuns, like Hildegard of Bingen he carefully covered over his antifeminism. Not a word was ever said about 'the receptacle of Satan'. On the contrary, the 'mellifluous' saint surpassed himself in courtesy and treated them as his equals. But when dealing with women of the lower class who had tagged on to wandering preachers and heretics, he behaved differently. If they were arrested, he recommended they be separated from the men and put into nunneries in order to observe whether they lived in chastity and also to provide them with witnesses of their lives as well as some supervision.[44]

This calls for several remarks. In the first place, it is taken for granted that Bernard is an 'antifeminist'. Then, the way he wrote to women is described at second-hand from one single—and very simplified—allusion by one single

---

[44]'Die Klassenposition Bernards drückte sich auch in seiner Einstellung zu den Frauen aus. Verkehrte er mündlich oder schriftlich mit Damen adeliger Herkunft oder Nonnen, wie Hildegard von Bingen, dann war nichts von seinem "Antifeminismus" zu verspüren, dann war keine Rede von "Gefässen des Satans" sondern der "honigfliessende" Heilige überschlug sich in Artigkeiten und erkannte sie als gleichstehend mit ihm an [note 381]. Ganz anders bei Frauen aus dem Volke, die sich Wanderpredigern oder Ketzern angeschlossen hatten. Wurden sie festgenommen, dann empfahl er sie von den Männern zu trennen, in Klöstern unterzubringen, um zu prüfen, ob sie keusch lebten, und ihnen auf diese Weise Zeugen und Wächter in einem zu geben [note 382]', E. Werner, *Stadt und Geistesleben im Hochmittelalter* (Leipzig, 1980) 149–150.

author.[45] Werner never quotes Bernard's own texts. Furthermore, the ironic use of the word 'mellifluous' is not in keeping with the way the word was sometimes used of Bernard.[46] And again, the expression 'vessel of Satan' or 'creature of Satan' is not to be found in Bernard's works.[47] Finally, it supposes that in the twelfth century there were only two kinds of women making up two social 'classes': on one hand, ladies and nuns, and on the other, common women. And of the second sort are mentioned only those who joined wandering preachers and representatives of the so-called popular heresies—which were, in fact, supported by numerous aristocrats—which went under various names, one of which was 'cathars'. For such women there was only one solution, according to Werner: an enforced monastic life.

These last assertions are based, it is claimed, on the final paragraph of Sermon 66 of the *Sermons on the Song*. In Sermons 65 and 66 Bernard had refuted the Rhineland heretics denounced by Eberwin of Steinfeld.[48] What does the text actually say when replaced in its context? From the start of the sermon Bernard speaks out against the condemnation such heretics levelled against certain foods and against marriage: *nuptias damnat*.[49] There follows a long statement, seven full pages, containing specific information and subtle variations about other errors on baptism and points of traditional christian teaching and about the deviations they can give rise to in practice. In fact, the rejection of 'honest marriage' seemed to lead to men and

---

[45]Note 381 refers to R. Manselli, 'San Bernardo e la religiosità popolare', in *Studi su San Bernardo di Chiaravalle nell'ottavo centenario della canonizzazione* (Rome, 1975) 258.

[46]'*Mellifluus*', in *Études sur saint Bernard*,184–191.

[47]R. Manselli, *loc.cit.*, wrote 'if a woman was not a nun, she tended to be a creature of Satan'.

[48] Note 382 refers to *Sermones super Cantica*, 66.14; II:187. On the origin of sermons 65 and 66, see *Recueil d'études sur saint Bernard* I:196–197.

[49] SC 66.3; II:179.

women living together and their 'habits of concubinage are a cause of scandal'. The practice was supported by certain members of the nobility, the clergy, and even the episcopate, who derive benefits from situations of this kind and receive presents from dissenters who carefully concealed their state of life. Bernard concluded:

They can easily be dealt with by this means, if by no other. As I have said, you must separate the men from the women, although they claim they are living chaste lives, and require the women to live with others of their sex who are under similar vows, and similarly men with men of the same way of life. In this way you will protect the vows and the reputations of both, and they will have you as witnesses and guardians of their chastity. If they do not accept this, you will be completely justified in expelling them from the Church to which they have caused scandal by their blatant and illicit cohabitation.[50]

It is hard to see in this text any encouragement for imposing monastic life on common women as a means of preventing class struggle.

5. *Women's Faith*

Since the problem of social class has been raised, it is quite legitimate for us to examine the sole documents mentioning the direct and immediate relations— we might even say the contacts—Bernard had with many women when he worked the miracles attributed to him. Two things seem to demand a certain reserve in this matter. On the one hand, it is not in Bernard's own writings that we read anything on the subject. And on the other hand, an historian ought to be prudent about facts he cannot verify

---

[50]SC 66.14; II:187; trans. Kilian Walsh, OCSO and Irene M. Edmonds, *On the Song of Songs* 3 (Kalamazoo: Cistercian Publications, 1979) 205–206.

or which arise from some literary genre and stress the unusual. Yet these extraordinary favors Bernard is supposed to have obtained for others, women in particular, have been advanced as evidence of his way of dealing with them.[51] We have, then, every right to take a closer look at them.

An inquiry of this kind is all the more justified in that, in Bernard's case, we have something exceptionally rare— depositions by persons who were his contemporaries and who relate, almost always briefly and soberly, events which they claim to have witnessed with their own eyes. Whatever may be of the historicity or the true nature— whether physiological or psychological—of the healings worked by Bernard, what we are told about the circumstances in which they took place already reveals the type of people who approached him. Here we shall consider only those 'miracles' about which his travelling companions made 'notes', a sort of log-book written up day by day. These reports deal with the stages of the abbot of Clairvaux's journeys in the east of France and in the Rhineland in 1146 and 1147, and before that in 1145, in the south of France. Taken together they make up what became Book VI of the *Vita prima*.[52] The interesting thing about them is that they were written by people who were with him: *Eramus autem cum eo . . . .*[53] Nearly a century later, the most reliable texts about Saint Francis of Assisi also began with the words: *Nos qui cum eo fuimus . . . . .*[54]

---

[51] E. Russel, 'Bernard et les dames de son temps', in *Bernard de Clairvaux*, p. 417.

[52] *PL* 185:373–416. On the origin and the history of this collection of miracles and the intentions which lay behind the collation of the anthology, see H.A. Bredero, '*Études sur la Vita prima de saint Bernard*', in *Analecta SOC* 17 (1961) 222–241.

[53] *Vita prima*, VI.I.1; *PL* 185.

[54] See R. Manselli, '*Nos qui cum eo fuimus*'. *Contributo alla questione francescana* (Rome, 1980).

According to these stories, people of all ages benefitted by Bernard's healing powers. We find a high proportion of children and persons from every social category. A typical passage concerns the town of Bragerach, and mentions in succession 'a nobleman', a 'poor beggar', and a 'servant of the bishop'.[55] About fifty percent of those cured by Bernard's miracles were women and they are often referred to as young girls (*puellae*), or adolescent girls, and even little girls (*puellulae*). An approximate reckoning shows that most cases concerned the blind—about thirty women and around ten young people; then the lame—about fifteen women and the same number of youngsters; after that, people with withered hands—ten women and seven young persons; finally, with one or two in each category of women and young people, paralytics and cripples, the deaf and the dumb, and deaf-mutes. One complex case concerned a 'young blind woman, limping on both feet, dumb and having a withered hand'.[56] Another woman suffered from headaches and still another was mentally ill. One woman, possessed by the devil, for whom Bernard showed concern, one evening asked that he come and heal her during the night. He gave her communion the next morning and she called him 'little abbot' (*abbaticulus*), which might be either a term of affection or, if inspired by the devil, ironic.[57] One mother presented her 'little girl',[58] another her 'child',[59] yet another her 'already grown up daughter'.[60] A father brought his paralyzed daughter. An epileptic woman presented her dumb daughter and asked that she be cured. Social rank is mentioned in these cases of healing no more of women than of men. The only two

[55] 411C.
[56] 377C.
[57] 414A.
[58] 404D.
[59] 416D.
[60] 392C.

instances where we find a member of the nobility referred to involve the 'sister of the advocate of Cologne'—and she is mentioned not because she herself was healed, but because of her deaf-mute child[61]—and an 'honored woman', niece of the count of Juilly.[62] Elsewhere, we find merely 'an honored and very well-known woman in the town who had been blind in one eye for five years and admitted to having spent a great deal of money, to no avail, on doctors'.[63] The word 'matron' is applied to a blind woman who is perhaps identical with the one just mentioned. The witness Gerard says that 'one of our brothers was astonished that a benefit be so easily accorded to a rich person'.[64] This monk of Clairvaux seems to suppose then that Bernard's favors were primarily for the poor. Yet, Bernard made no discrimination. Another 'rich matron, well-known in the town, had been obliged to keep to her bed for the last three years'.[65] Geoffrey of Auxerre does not specify the social standing of the woman, whom he calls 'the niece of our hostess'.[66]

All other women miraculously healed seem to have belonged to the common people. One blind woman was a beggar.[67] A crippled woman was 'fed by the nuns in the church of Saint Mary'.[68] Various other women who are said to be 'known' among the people were known because they were infirm or handicapped or had had, for example, to be carried for many years on a pallet.[69] One day, when three women had been healed, 'Count Thibaut and many

---

[61]391D.
[62]393A.
[63]390B.
[64]390C–D.
[65]389C.
[66]377B.
[67]401A.
[68]403D.
[69]405D; 399C; 403C.

others, nobles and others, were present'.[70] It appears from all these accounts that each one, man and woman alike, had easy access to Bernard, who blessed them and often touched them, and whose interventions caused enthusiasm among the crowds. The people acclaimed him and crowded round him so much that he had difficulty getting back to the place he was staying.[71] He sometimes took the opportunity of these walk-abouts to bring people back to the church, where they gave thanks to God.

One conversation related by Gerard is worth our attention if we are interested in the sociological aspect of these stories.

> Anselm, bishop of Havelberg, had such a headache and such a sore throat that he could hardly swallow anything at all, So he implored the blessed man [Bernard], saying 'You ought to heal me too'. To which Bernard replied jokingly (*iucunde*): 'If you had as much faith as these simple women, maybe it would help you!' And the bishop retorted: 'Well, even if I have no faith, let your faith save me' Finally the father [Bernard] made the sign of the cross over him, touched him, and immediately all the pain left him as well as any sign of swelling.[72]

The word used in this passage for the miraculously healed women is a diminutive *mulierculae*, which can mean either a small woman or one of lowly condition, i.e. a woman of the people.[73] The context tends to give the impression that it is this latter meaning which is implied here. When we realize that Anselm of Havelberg, a Premonstratensian canon, was then not only a bishop, but also a writer and

---

[70]404C.

[71]391C, etc.

[72]384C.

[73]See below, the Excursus 'The meaning of adiminutive applied to women'.

well-known theologian,[74] we can appreciate the contrast
Bernard drew between the prelate-teacher and a humble
woman with stronger faith. This short story gives us some
idea of the good humor which prevailed among those 'who
were with Saint Bernard',[75] even, and especially, it seems
when he had done good to some woman.

### 6. *Women and Satan.*

At the beginning of an essay entitled *Le moine et la femme*,
in the vocabulary of twelfth-century religious art, one historian has written:

> For the monk, woman is nearly as fearsome as the
> demon. She is his instrument, and he makes use of
> her to bring saints to perdition. Such is the feeling of
> the great abbots, reformers of the monastic life. They
> are all afraid of women; they do not want the monk to
> expose himself to temptation, only too sure he will
> succumb. To live with a woman without danger, says
> Saint Bernard, is more difficult than to raise a dead
> man to life.[76]

---

[74]On Anselm, bishop of Havelberg, 1129–1155, then archbishop and
exarch of Ravenna until his death in 1158, and on his writings, see J.W.
Braun, art. 'Anselm von Havelberg', in *Lexikon des Mittelalters*, I
(Munich-Zurich, 1980) col. 678–679.

[75]384A.

[76]Emile Mâle, *L'art religieux du XII<sup>e</sup> siècle en France. Études sur les origines
de l'iconographie du Moyen Age* (Paris, 1922) p. 373. The title *Le moine et la
femme* is given in the *Table générale des matières*, p. 459. Other texts,
quoted on p. 373, are given either without taking their context into
consideration, or else at second hand; a mention of monks at the mill is
not justified by any reference. Later on, A. Fliche, writing about saint
Bernard, said 'La femme lui est toujours apparue comme l'incarnation
du démon', 'Du premier concile du Latran à l'avènement d'Innocent III
(1123–1198)', in *Histoire de l'église publiée sous la direction de A. Fliche et V.
Martin*, IX (Paris, 1948) 107. 'La femme "organe du diable" selon saint
Bernard', J.M. Aubert, *Antiféminisme et christianisme* (Paris, 1975) p. 338.

These last words are given without any reference to the work from which they were taken. In fact, the text modifies a phrase of sermon 65.4 *On the Song of Songs,* written in refutation of the Rhineland heretics whom we described above.[77] Bernard thought they allowed marriage by cohabitation between spouses but without marital relations. Some even taught that marriage should be contracted only between two virgins, who intended to remain so after marriage, even though living together. In such a situation, declared Bernard in a statement many profane authors would readily have signed, continence is almost impossible. What Bernard actually says is: 'Is it not more difficult to be always with a woman and not couple with her, than to raise a dead man to life?' He specifically says that this mutual closeness continues every moment, day and night. This does not refer either to monks or to married people living a normal marital life. In the entire context Bernard makes no allusion to the devil. Nor does he say anywhere else, as has been suggested, that woman is either a 'receptacle of satan' or a 'creature' of anyone but God alone.

We see then how the association between woman and the demon was first made in the minds of people who then projected their opinion onto Saint Bernard, from whose works it is entirely absent.

---

[77] SC 65.II:175. On this sermon see above. On marriage between virgins SC 66.4; II:180.

# CHAPTER VII

# SAINT BERNARD AND THE MISOGYNISTS OF HIS DAY

*1. Evidence of Misogyny.*

T HE TIME HAS COME for us to discern whether or not Bernard was a misogynist and, if he was, to what extent. We can only judge by comparing him with other men of his day who, if we believe their texts, were, or were considered to be, women-haters. A comparative enquiry of this sort would prove enormous and it is surely not possible until each author has been examined very minutely. There are, in fact, a few overviews but we lack the monographs we need to be able to draw up a synthesis. Even so, we may at least attempt to situate Saint Bernard in the context of what we already know provisionally. A first inventory, which though written some sixty years ago is still helpful, is the work of A. Wulff, *Die fraufeindlichen Dichtungen in den romanischen Literaturen des Mittelalters bis zum Ende des XIII. Jahrhunderts.*[1] This is a partial work in both

---

[1] A. Wulff, *Die fraufeindlichen Dichtungen in den romanischen Literaturen des Mittelalters bis zum Ende des XIII. Jahrhunderts*, 2 vols, with continuous pagination (Halle, 1914). Other witnesses have been cited by various historians; for example, M. Manitius, *Geschichte der lateinischen Literatur des Mittelalters*, III (Munich, 1971) 880; E. Hermes, *The 'Disciplina Clericalis' of Petrus Alfonsi* (London-Henley, 1977) 5 and 13. The work of Katherine M. Rogers, *The Troublesome Helpmate. A History of Misogyny in Literature* (Seattle-London, 1966) deals with a thousand years of the

'Middle Ages' in forty-three pages (56–99), and contains only two short senses of the word: partial because since it came out many other studies have appeared on texts which have been discovered and edited; partial too in the sense that Wulff confined his study to polemical writings, leaving to one side the host of other works devoid of combative viewpoints. His work needs to be completed on many points. That it should be a 'partial' work is only to be expected: when specializing in this sort of document one always tends to fall into the temptation of exaggerating its importance.

His long introduction[2] devoted to pre-christian greek and latin, and then to patristic literature, gives the impression that antifeminism was widespread, dominant, and unvarying. Yet someone thoroughly familiar with every aspect of the study of women in antiquity, K. Thraede, makes no more than a passing allusion to it[3] and contents himself with referring to a work containing a bibliography on it.[4] But on the other hand, he does deal with several

---

references to the twelfth century in connection with John of Salisbury and Andrew the Chaplain. The enquiry is moreover limited to works of 'literature', to the exclusion of other witnesses to real life, and to English and American authors.

[2]Wulff, 1–8.

[3]K. Thraede, art. 'Frau', in *Reallexicon für Antike und Christentum*, VIII (Stuttgart, 1972) col. 197–269. To be completed for the Bible by K.H. Scheckle, *Der Geist und die Braut. Die Frauen der Bibel* (Düsseldorf, 1977) with general bibliography, p. 12, and special bibliographies at the beginning of each chapter dealing with a book or a passage of the Bible, and J.H. Otwell, *And Sarah Laughed. The Status of Women in the Old Testament* (Philadelphia, 1977). To other ancient witnesses we may add the little poem on woman, probably inspired by Proverbs 5, to be found in Michelini Tocci, *I manoscritti del Mar Morto* (Bari, 1967) 355–359: 'Poemetto sulla donna'. On the part played by woman in the 'Traductions et adaptations de l'Ancien Testament en anglais', see M.M. Lares, in *The Bible in the Middle Ages* (Louvain, 1979) 79–80.

[4]Thraede, col. 221, refers to D.S. Wiesen, *St Jerome as a Satirist. A Study in Christian Latin Thought and Letters* (Ithaca, 1964). On the classical tradition on which Saint Jerome depended, see also P. Antin, *Saint Jérôme. Sur Jonas*, Sources chrétiennes, 43 (Paris, 1956) 25. Presenting

'Un témoin de l'antiféminisme au XIIIe siècle', in *Revue bénédictine* 80
other aspects of the question: the position of women in
political, economic, social, cultural, artistic, familial, philo-
sophic, moral, and religious life. Wulff is interesting because he reminds us that the antifeministic bias is attested
to in the most ancient cultures known, some of which—
India, for example—may perhaps have had some influence
on the writings and mentality of the Middle Ages. In greek
literature, from Hesiod in the seventh century BC to the
christian era, we meet with all themes which crop up later
on: the contemptible nature of the female creature, her
vices, and especially the failings of wives, and satires on
feminine dress. The poet Semonides, from Amorgos, in
the seventh century BC, had already gone so far as to
compose a *Mirror for Women*, a long poem of 118 verses. The
patristic writers had practically nothing to add, save the
theme of Eve, the first *femme fatale*. Among the latins we
find a rival tendency to shower abuse on women in poets
like Catullus, Virgil, Propertius, Ovid, Juvenal, and in
philosophers like Seneca, not to mention the grammarians
Quintilian and Fulgentius. Christian writers illustrated old
commonplaces with new examples taken from the Bible.[5]
Saint Jerome, for example, whom we may rightly reproach
for his acid comments about roman women,[6] appears to
have been less of a woman hater than an opponent of
marriage—though he, along with the rest of the Church,
was sometimes obliged to defend it. To sum up briefly,

---

(1970) 304–307, I have already quoted a few works before the publication
of this article. Useful on Saint Jerome in particular, in addition to
Wiesen, are the works of P. Delhaye, 'Le dossier antimatrimonial de l'
"Adversus Jovinianum" et son influence sur quelques écrits latins du
XIIe siècle', in *Medieval Studies* 13 (1955) 71–75; P. Antin, *Essai sur saint
Jérôme* (Paris, 1951) 81–83, 197–203; *Recueil sur saint Jérôme* (Brussels, 1968)
467, Index, at the word *Femme*.

[5]On John Chrysostom in particular, we now have at our disposal the
well-informed and nuanced essay of Cantalessa, concerning especially
pre-christian greek sources: *Etica sessuale nel matrimonio cristiano delle
origini* (Milan, 1976) 332.

[6]The formula is from Wiessen, p. 127.

everything had already been said on this theme in literary tradition: there was nothing left for the Middle Ages to invent, which is why it was so 'unoriginal'.

When dealing with this, Wulff depends mainly on texts edited by T. Wright (*Womankind in Western Europe from the Earliest Times Till the XVIIth Century*), and this restricts his study because Wright was interested only in satire.[7] Wulff also takes a look at texts edited by Ménil (*Poésies populaires latines antérieures au XIIᵉ siècle*) who did no more than collate 'popular poems'.[8] We could add to this list countless hymns and canticles, both liturgical and devotional, which would undoubtedly modify the image transmitted by the satiric and popular genres. Among the poets of the early years of the twelfth century there was Marbode of Rennes who, at the advanced age of 67, wrote eighty-nine hexameters for clerics with the aim of convincing them of the advantages of celibacy. Yet he does not fail, in another work, to sing the praises of the virtuous wife.[9] Hildebert of Lavardin, who died as Bishop of Le Mans in 1135, also had something to say to consecrated men (*sacris hominibus*) to dissuade them from taking wives. He describes all the inconveniences of having a wife but his vituperations are not so much about women as about the temptation some clerics felt to get married.[10] Bernard of Morlas, who seems to have been getting at monks and nuns of the order of Cluny, showed he had a real 'hatred of the fair sex'. His main source is the Sixth Satire of Juvenal and the Proverbs attributed to Solomon, and to these he had nothing new to

---

[7]T. Wright, *Womankind in Western Europe from the Earliest Times till the X VIIth Century* (London, 1969).

[8]E. du Ménil, *Poésies populaires latines antérieures au XIIᵉ siècle* (Paris, 1845).

[9]Wulff, 20–22.

[10]*Ibid.*, 22–24. Cf. also P. von Moos, *Hildebert von Lavardin. 1056–1153* (Stuttgart, 1965) 18–19, 208–239: 'Frau. Ehe und Liebe'.

contribute.[11] At the end of the century, Alexander Neckham ( + 1217), in a work *On the Life of the Monk*, expressed himself with the same intention and in the same vein as the foregoing writers, composing sixty antifeminist distiches that is, 120 verses.[12] Among the minor poets—authors of moralizing texts or of proverbs—Wulff quotes some who have left us tirades of twenty-six, forty-nine or more than sixty verses.[13] To these we find added a first-class writer, Abelard, with his *Lament on Samson*.[14] This looks like a very severe text, but Peter Dronke has managed to interpret it optimistically.[15]

Abelard was also, and before all else, a prose writer: the teaching on woman and womankind we find in his letters and his theological works would be worth going into more deeply. But it already appears that while his letters, especially Letter Seven, reveal a practical and favorable attitude towards women, his speculative teaching does so far less.[16] Peter Alphonsus, in his *Discipline for the Clergy*, exploits the

---

[11]Wulff, 24–28. The author has been identified as Bernard de Morlas, or Morval, or 'the Cluniac', in *Dictionnaire des lettres françaises, Moyen Age*, and Manitius, III:780–783. His *De contemptu mundi* has been edited by H.C. Hoskins (London, 1929). See also P.C. Perry, 'Medieval Eschatology and Social Responsibility in Bernard of Morval's "De contemptu mundi"', in *Speculum* 24 (1949) 207–217.

[12]Wulff, 28–32.

[13]*Ibid.*, 44–53.

[14]*Ibid.*, 41.

[15]Peter Droncke, 'Peter Abelard: Planctus and Satire', in *Poetic Individuality in the Middle Ages. New Departures in Poetry 1000–1050* (Oxford, 1970) 114–145.

[16]On the feminism of Abelard in his letters see 'Ad ipsam sophiam Christum. Le témoignage monastique d'Abélard', in *Revue d'ascétique et de mystique*, 40 (1970) 161–181. On his doctrine, see R. Javelet, *Image et ressemblance au XII<sup>e</sup> siècle* (Paris, 1967) I:241: 'Il apparaît que l'amant d'Héloïse était moins féministe que la plupart des auteurs sapirituels'. On the complexity of Abelard's thought, as it is expressed in his works, including his hymns, in which woman is both symbol and reality, see G. Lodolo, 'Il segno della donna nel medioevo', in *Aevum* 51 (1971) 28.

antifeminist theme for purposes of moralizing.[17] The virulent misogyny of the last section of Andrew the Chaplain's *Art of Courtly Love* is well-known.[18] These texts do not, of course, give a complete picture of the attitude thinkers of those days held of women. A comprehensive view can only be obtained by examining the immense fields of canonical, theological, and spiritual literature. This more austere type of literature has been thoroughly read and summarized by M. Bernards in works which have not yet been sufficiently exploited.[19]

From romance literature, Wulff has picked out from the twelfth century a few 'sayings' and *fabliaux*, though these genres developed only later on.[20] Likewise, expressions of declared antifeminism in courtly poems are relatively rare in comparison with what the next and following centuries were to produce. A noteworthy exception is a monk of Montaudon who alternated between life as a troubadour and stays in priories until his death in the first years of the thirteenth century. He has bequeathed us two 'tensons'—one of seventy-eight verses, the other of eighty-five—both of them 'satires against women'.[21] *Fabliaux* and other poems influenced the literature of the following period regarding women and marriage.[22]

We could quote other twelfth-century witnesses: the twenty or so anonymous lines denouncing the danger to clerics of having long conversations (*confabulatio*) with

---

[17]Wulff, 63–65.

[18]*Ibid.*, 65–72.

[19]For example, 'Die Welt der Laien in der Kölnischen Theologie des 12. Jahrhunderts. Beobachtungen zur Ekklesiologie Ruperts von Deutz', in *Die Kirche und ihre Amter und Stände, Festgabe J. Frings* (1960) 415.

[20]Wulff, 103–137.

[21]*Ibid.*, 169–172.

[22]G.R. Mermier, 'D'un chapitre du 'De miseria humanae conditionis' du pape Innocent III aux "Quinze joies du mariage" ', in H. Niedzielski, ed., *Studies on the Seven Sages of Rome and other Essays in Medieval Literature dedicated to Jean Misrahi* (Honolulu, 1978) 243–247.

women contained in the *Miscellanea* in the appendix to the
works of Hugh of Saint Victor;[23] the short treatises of Hugh
of Fouilloy on the 'fleshly nuptials to be avoided' and the
spiritual to be embraced;[24] then, at the end of the century,
pages by Cardinal Lothair, the future Innocent III, in his
work *On the Misery of the Human Condition*.[25]

John of Salisbury deserves attention because he passes
as one of the greatest humanists of the twelfth century and
was a contemporary of Bernard, although his junior by a
whole generation. Born sometime around 1115, John lived
and studied in France, under Abelard, from 1136 to 1148. He
was in Rome when Bernard died. He ended his life as
Bishop of Chartres from 1176 to 1180. In his compendium of
political knowledge, the *Polycraticus*, he devotes a very
long chapter to criticizing and even satirizing the state of
matrimony and, in this connection, woman.[26] He lauds the
philosopher who remains single. What interested John was
not clerical or religious celibacy, but the bachelor state of
that wise man, the sage, who avoids women for the sake of
wisdom. It is indeed rare, he thought, to find a man who
possesses wisdom! Like many other authors, he quotes a
verse from Juvenal, completely altering its meaning. What
in the poet was satire against an honest but tedious

---

[23]*PL* 177:588 C-D, in the chapter entitled *De contemptu mundi inducendo.*
On the authors of the texts which make up the whole collection, see H.
Rochais, 'Les Miscellanea et les Sentences de saint Bernard', in *Analecta*,
18 (1962) 148–151. The danger of *confabulatio* was felt by every man and
woman, including married women, as in the case of Guibert of Nogent's
mother, as has been shown in an excellent introduction by John F.
Benton dealing with this sort of problem: *Self and Society in Medieval
France, The Memoirs of Abbot Guibert of Nogent* (New York-Evanston, 1970)
6–33.

[24]*De nuptiis carnalibus vitandis . . . De nuptiis spiritalibus amplexandis*, *PL*
176:1201–1218.

[25]*De miseria humanae conditionis*, I,17:'De miseria continentis et con-
iugati', ed. M. Maccarone (Lugano, 1955).

[26]*Polycraticus*, VIII.II.

woman,[27] becomes an argument for proving that hardly a single modest woman exists. John closes with brief praise for such a woman, when he might chance to come across one. But this follows a long diatribe of several pages against womankind in general and practically against every woman. He quotes Epicurus, Theophrastus, Heroditus, Cicero, the roman philosophers and satirists and, of course, Saint Jerome.

All this seems overwhelming. But one historian has done his best to show that when John of Salisbury is compared with the authors to whom he refers, he distinguishes himself as a moderate misogynist.[28] Perhaps so. But, what is important is not that he is less virulent than his sources, but that he takes his inspiration precisely from those sources and no other. This is also evident when we examine, for example, his correspondence. In the excellent *Index* which C.N.L. Brooke has drawn up at the end of the second volume of the critical edition of his letters, we notice that John of Salisbury quotes Ovid more than thirty times, Juvenal more than twenty; there are several dozen references to the wisdom books attributed to Solomon, especially Proverbs and Ecclesiasticus, but only three references to the Song of Songs[29] where woman is described and praised, and which Bernard and those who continued his writings took such delight in. John mentions this book of the Bible only in the context of a brief and learned discussion about the authenticity of works attributed to Solomon.[30]

---

[27]*Satirae*, VI.165.

[28]J. van Laarhoven, in *Nederlands Archiev voor Kerkgeschiedenis*. According to K.M. Rogerts, p. 57, the *Polycraticus* is a 'miscellany intended as joyous entertainment' an entertainment, significantly, at the expense of women.

[29]*The Letters of John of Salisbury*, vol II, ed. by W.G. Millor and revised by C.N.L. Brooke (Oxford, 1979) 817.

[30]*Ibid.*, Millor-Brooke, *letter 209*; 328–329.

## 2. *The Content and Confines of Misogyny.*

If, having now gone through some of the antifeminist texts of the twelfth century—and there are others besides those cited here—, we attempt to highlight the major features we find there, several things stand out about the number of these works, their literary genre, their purpose and content.

First of all, can we rightly say that these texts are 'legion'?[31] Certainly there is no dearth of them. But as in antiquity, so in the Middle Ages: when these texts are set among all the literary works produced on subjects other than women and against women, they are in the minority. Furthermore, examination of the manuscript tradition of most of them would show that they had a limited diffusion[32]: many have been preserved in merely a few, sometimes late, manuscripts, or even in a single manuscript.[33]

In the case of the *Polycraticus* of John of Salisbury, we have on this point a well documented study[34] whose author, A. Linder, shows that the work, completed in 1159 (that is to say, a few years after Saint Bernard's death) circulated far less than did Bernard's works during his own lifetime and immediately after his death in 1153. There were hundreds of bernardine manuscripts, many of them monastic, copied throughout the twelfth century and up to about the middle of the thirteenth. But circulation of John of Salisbury's treatise 'remained rather limited', to about a dozen manuscripts before 1180. 'Throughout the whole of the thirteenth century, the dissemination of the *Polycraticus* was still a very slow process, and its actual study and

---

[31]Wulff, p. 57.

[32]This is the case, for example, of the *De amore* of Andrew the Chaplain and of most of the fabliaux. See *Monks on Marriage* 66–67.

[33]This is what is evident from indications given by Ph. Menard, *Fabliaux français du Moyen Age. Edition critique* (Geneva, 1979) 129–168.

[34]A. Linder, 'John of Salisbury's Manuscripts', in *Studi medievali*, 3rd series, 18/2 (1977) 315–366.

secondary use remained rather limited'. Indeed, 'The introduction of pagan classical literature to the curriculum of the faculties of Arts created a demand among lecturers and students for information about the pagan philosophers and their schools'. And so it was that extracts from the *Polycraticus* began to be included in compilations, especially for the use of the mendicant Orders who found these selected passages, often in the form of *exempla*, useful in their preaching.

Thus, while the monks continued to read the works of Saint Bernard, the mendicants resorted to these anthologies. It is only from the fourteenth century onwards that John of Salisbury's treatise began to enjoy a certain popularity: it was then that it crossed over from England to the Continent. Even so, interest centered less on the text itself than on extracts or *Tables* and *Indexes* of various names summarizing the content and intended more often for the use of jurists than of theologians, lay humanists than clerics. For the twelfth and thirteenth centuries, the only author in whose writings it has been possible to identify quotations from John of Salisbury's chapter about the inconveniences of marriage and the failings of women is Lothair of Segni in his treatise *On the Misery of the Human Condition*. This restricts still more the circles in which this passage of the *Polycraticus* was diffused.

The anti-feminist writings of the twelfth century are often quite long poems, with many verses, and they catch the attention of historians. Sometimes they are merely a series of proverbs strung together. Generally they depend on the satirical genre, and, as easily happens in this area, tend to become caricatures. Their authors quite unrealistically seem not to have observed how real women in their surroundings actually lived. These men tirelessly and rather monotonously simply recopied one another or else cribbed from the same anthologies.

Most wrote with a moralizing, even a reforming purpose, except for those *salsa dicta*[35] intended as distractions for students. Sometimes they warn all men about the danger of all women—virgins, wives, widows, nuns—, and sometimes they are aimed at clerics and monks who have voluntarily taken it upon themselves to live in celibacy. In the first case, belittling marriage goes hand in hand with belittling women in general. They fling all sorts of insults at her: she is compared to animals like the lioness, the tigress; she smells foul; she is poison, or the symbol of everything evil in the world.[36] She has every vice and every failing, and one in particular: her tongue is evil, garrulous, deceitful, flattering, lying. Women cheat in every possible way: they are duplicitous and fickle, in marriage and out of marriage; they are never to be trusted. The best thing to do is to avoid marrying.

While all this was being written, any man who could marry did marry, while many women chose monastic celibacy and remained faithful to it. Real life was quite different from the picture given by these obviously artificial texts. They give us neither a true image of life as it really was, nor a correct doctrine— or, as we say today, a feminine anthropology. These writings were no more than slick literature which saved the authors the trouble of having to be creative, because the commonplaces they used were within easy reach of anyone, either in anthologies or in school day memories. One of the dearest themes of antifeminist satire always has been, and still is, perfumes, cosmetics, make-up, outlandish fashions.[37]

To illustrate all these physical and psychological shortcomings, the mythology and literature of ancient Greece

---

[35] Wulff, p. 58.

[36]This theme has been studied particularly by W. Stammler, *Frau Welt. Eine mittelalterliche Allegorie* (Freiburg-im-Breisgau, 1959); for the period which interests us here, see pp. 9–20.

[37]Thraede, 'Frau', col. 223–224, 251–252.

and Rome offer many examples: the chimera, the wife of Charybdis, Circe in the *Odyssey*, Paris and Hippolytus, Helen Theophrastus, Hannibal ruled by women in the midst of the delights of Capua. Were we to turn to the Bible, we could easily condemn Eve, the mother of all evils; Dalila who stole away Samson's strength; Uriah's wife with whom David committed adultery; the wives and concubines among whom Solomon lost his wisdom; Job's wife who heaped reproach on him; and finally, texts like Ecclesiastes, chapter 7, verse 29, which opens with an exaggerated formula: 'Among all who please God I find one man in a thousand, but of all women, I find not a single one'. And then, in the Gospel, do we not read that it was a woman, Salome, who arranged the beheading of John the Baptist? All this pre-christian and biblical data was orchestrated by Saint Jerome. And these were the sources, easily accessible to all: anyone could dip into them, and there were many who seized the opportunity. What position did Bernard take with regard to this tradition and the ease with which some of his contemporaries used it?

### 3. *Saint Bernard's Position.*

Having pointed it out above, we need not repeat everything positive and favorable in Bernard's attitude to womankind and women. But now that we have brought up all the negative and unfavorable features in authors before Bernard, or contemporary with him, we can sum up all the things we do *not* find in his writings about women.

First of all, nowhere do we find long pages of tedious tirades against women. Yet, as we know, Bernard excelled in the art of satire—he proved it in the *Apologia*[38]—and in caricature, which we find in the treatise *On the Steps of Humility*, and elsewhere.[39] But never do we find him doing this when writing about women.

---

[38]'Un modèle du genre satirique' in *Recueil* III (Rome, 1969) 45–54.
[39]*Ibid.*, 116–117.

In particular we find no description of the ridiculous way women dressed. He twice mentions the feminine fashions of his day but, in one case, it is in order to criticize men—prelates and knights—, and in the other, it occurs in one of the two texts where he considers the ornaments with which women deck themselves as a means of showing and deepening their marital affection, and this justifies it.[40] This absence of satire against female dress is still more remarkable in that Bernard knew Saint Jerome's purple piece on the subject and he did take inspiration from one of Jerome's formulas there, but again, it was to denounce masculine abuses. In his letter 22 to Eustochium, Jerome included a couplet against the luxurious way women dressed, used make-up and had expensive manuscripts decorated for their personal use: 'Books are clothed in precious stones while Christ is dying, naked, at their doors'.[41] In the *Apologia*, Bernard, writing of cluniac churches, says 'The church walls glow, but its poor go hungry. It covers its stones with gold, but leaves its children naked'.[42] And then he goes on immediately to develop his theme at some length. He could have done the same about women!

In Bernard's works we find no lists of all those vices and shortcomings of which some supposed women uniquely capable. The notion of the 'weaker sex' is taken for granted, and sometimes mentioned in passing, but without the stress given it by other writers. Nor do we find any reminders of the evil attributed to women frequently in mythology and ancient greek and latin literature, in which Jerome found his inspiration, so eagerly echoed by the misogynists of the twelfth century.

Again, of the various biblical themes which shower abuse upon women, we find not a single one in Bernard.

---

[40]See above, n. 21.
[41]Ep 22.32; quoted by Wiesen, p. 127.
[42]Apo 28; III:105–106.

Eve is never, as we have seen, accused of being the only, nor even the principal, cause of the first sin. On the contrary, she is excused and the major responsibility for this first fault is laid on Adam. Likewise, Solomon's fall is attributed, not to his wives and concubines, but to luxury (1 K 11:1–3), and it is David, not Uriah's wife, who was guilty of adultery.

Finally, in Bernard's works we find never a warning against women in general, but merely a few practical cautions addressed to clerics and monks about keeping company with women. The lesson given clerics in the treatise *On Conversion* has a very general character and is part of a very much broader ascetical teaching: the feminine danger is only one, and not the most important factor.[43] As for the monks, those in question belong to three particular monasteries. Bernard never took the trouble to develop a general doctrine or program in this matter. Especially after the gregorian reforms caution about women was part of a systematic movement to encourage celibacy among clerics who had promised to observe it.[44] Any such preoccupation seems to be absent from Bernard's writings.

Now, all the themes and the arguments put forward against women before Bernard's day and during his lifetime were known to every writer. William of Saint Thierry, for example, knew about the 'bag of excrement'. If Bernard refrained from using these commonplaces, it was because he actively refused to use them. Yet, on the other hand, he liked to mention women whose words and conduct were worthy of admiration. There are many examples. Without giving the full statistics, we can pin-point a few cases

---

[43]'Aggressivité et répression chez Bernard de Clairvaux', in *Revue d'histoire de la spiritualité* 52 (1976) 155–172.

[44]A single example will suffice: William of Malmesbury, *Gesta Pontificum Anglorum* IV, ed. N. Hamilton (London, 1870) 327, describing the abbey of Thorney, writes: 'Femina ibi, si visitur, monstrum habetur, maribus advenientibus quasi angelis plaudetur'. It is easy to see the exaggeration in such a sentence.

scattered throughout his works. The Canticle of Deborah, in chapter five of the Book of Judges, is quoted and praised five times; Judith is ranked with the prophets (SC 1.7; I:6,2–3); the mother of the Maccabees is proposed as a model of heroism four times; there are sixty-five citations and reminiscences from chapter 13 of the Book of Daniel, which tells of the victory of the chaste Susannah over shameless old men. We find eighteen references to that page of the Gospel according to Saint Matthew (15:22–28) which mentions the Canaanite woman whose faith Jesus admired. Magdalen, the model of a converted and loving sinful woman, is always contrasted with the proud Pharisee who considers himself righteous. And Bernard even seems to have taken a certain pleasure in transforming the significance of certain biblical women: Sarah, who had doubts when Abraham was told she would bear him a son in her old age, becomes the symbol of faith (S II.130; VI/2:48,20). Elsewhere, the fact that her name was changed from Sarai to Sarah is used to suggest what conversion means for everyone, and what conversion meant for Eugene III, a monk become pope (Ep 238.2; VIII:116,16–18). What is more, Bernard suggests all this with a sense of humor which signals a healthy attitude rather than repression. To put it briefly, not only does Bernard not heap abuse on women when mentioning those in the Bible, but he even tends to admire them.

## 4. *Why is Bernard not a Misogynist?*

It is still not easy to answer this question. The problem is complex and every personality, especially a personality as rich as Saint Bernard's, remains a mystery. Several conjectures come to mind and probably each offers a partial solution.

First, it is well-known that Bernard took pains to be original in his writings. He was a great artist. Even when dealing with so hackneyed a subject as the panegyric for a deceased brother, as he did in his twenty-sixth sermon *On*

*the Song of Songs*, he renewed it: the criticism made on this
point by Beranger of Poitiers is groundless, and posterity
has sided against him.[45] Now, as we have seen, though it
was perhaps not very frequent it was at least fairly common, and very easy, to compose satire against women:
tradition had accumulated abundantly monotonous material. And there is nothing strange in the fact that a writer of
genius like Bernard should show his freedom in not giving
in to literary demands which had ensnared even someone
like John of Salisbury.

Furthermore, surely we can discern in the two types of
literature produced on the theme of women a mirroring of
two psychological attitudes which have been described
elsewhere. For our present purpose we merely recall that
traditional monasticism recruited mainly children offered
very young by their parents. But members of the new
Orders, Cistercians as well as others, were young adults,
often members of the aristocracy, raised in castles and
conversant beyond their years with the opposite sex, marriage, and love.[46]

To these differences in psychological and spiritual ap-
proach we must add the variety of motivations among the
writers themselves; those from traditional monasticism
were well aware of the danger that attraction to women
could pose to former oblates. Moralists and preachers
knew that clerics were exposed to loss of celibacy and
laymen tempted to infidelity to marriage ties. An author
like Bernard was addressing a public, mainly monastic,
which was thought to have overcome these difficulties,
and gone on to others. As he stated clearly at the beginning
of his *Sermons on the Song of Songs*, he had in mind readers
who had outgrown childhood and attained the maturity of
adulthood.[47] This may be applied to all his works, with the

---

[45]*Recueil d'études sur saint Bernard*, III:90–94.
[46]*Monks and Love*, 8–26.
[47]SC 1.12; I:8.

specifics mentioned above in connection with the treatise *On Conversion*. Certainly Bernard proposed to ordinary monks what we might call 'everyday mysticism', meaning that he did not ordinarily deal with sublime and exceptional experiences.[48] But he always treated spirituality and not fundamental morality, which he assumed had already been acquired.

Is it true that courtly literature of the period exerted some influence on Bernard and led him to tend to idealize women? He must have known about some romances: his whole milieu was permeated with it, and certain themes which he has in common with romantic literature have been detected in his works.[49] We know full well that this sort of literature was far from always idealizing woman,[50] but Bernard neither praised nor spurned her as these texts did, depending on their author. He made a critical allusion to authors of profane love songs,[51] and denounced monks who boasted of having once taken pleasure in such literature, even of having composed some of it.[52] Though he caricatured the 'knights of the world', we notice he said nothing about their ladies.

The decisive difference between Bernard and the misogynists of his day seems to derive from the sources on

---

[48]'Une mystique practique dans les sermons de saint Bernard à ses moines', in *Studia missionalia* 26 (1977) 73–86.

[49]J.P. Yh. Deroy, 'Thèmes et termes de la fin'amor dans les Sermones super Cantica canticorum de saint Bernard de Clairvaux', in *Actes du XI II^e Congrès international de linguistique et philologie romanes*, Université Laval (Québec, 1976) 853–867.

[50] And in fact, this literature in which women were frequently honored by poets was always a literature written only for men in a man's world; 'it does not favour an authentic respect for women as individuals'; this comes from John F. Benton, 'Clio and Venus: An Historical View of Medieval Love', in *The Meaning of Courtly Love, Papers. . .* edited by F-X. Newman (Albany, 1968) 19–42. Other opinions given by historians could be quoted in the same way.

[51]SC 74.I; II:239,25–240,1.

[52]SC 16.9; I:94.

which they depended. The seculars—ecclesiastics like John of Salisbury, perhaps Andrew the Chaplain, or laymen like the troubadours and writers of *fabliaux*—took their inspiration from two different traditions, the one biblical and patristic, the other profane and even pagan in the sense that it was foreign to christian faith, a tradition handed down by authors of classical antiquity. As someone has written, 'troubadour misogyny draws on the quite varying sources of greco-latin culture'.[53] This is true of all secular authors, even of clerics and bishops. But for Bernard of Clairvaux, who represents reformed claustral literature, the matter was different: his sources were biblical and patristic. Not that he and other monks were ignorant of classical literature. They quote from it, but less often than do seculars, and this may prove simply that they were less bookish, for we do in fact find in Bernard's writings enough reminiscences of profane writers to justify the observation that he did know them.[54] Ought we to go so far as to say that he rejected them and refused to use them? It would seem likelier that he felt no need to use them: his style was fashioned by the Bible, the liturgy, and the Fathers. These were enough for him.

And again, among them, he made selections. From Jerome he took only what he wanted and nothing which could have served to ridicule women. From Scripture he showed a preference for women worthy of admiration. Is there an explanation for this? Bernard got most of his Bible from the liturgy. In worship God is praised for all his marvelous deeds, including those he worked through the mediation of women or because of them. This is a contemplative rather than a moralizing attitude, and it results, not in bad examples to be avoided, but images of woman to be imitated, which shows what a woman is capable of doing

---

[53]J. Cheverny, *Sexologie de l'Occident* (Paris, 1976) 118.

[54]*Receuil d'études sur saint Bernard*, III: 68–72; on *De conversione* see above.

as well as, and sometimes better than, a man. Among women of this type there are some who prophesied and whose canticles are still sung by the Church. Others accomplished great deeds in the history of Israel, and still others were pardoned by the Lord Jesus because they were both humble and loving. The feminine image given by the liturgy matches exactly what we find in Bernard's writings.

The cumulative effect of these many possible influences is a theology which, in dealing with women, as with every other subject, is distinguished from the theology of moralists or speculative thinkers, without however being disconnected from it.[55] Saint Bernard did not dwell on the psychological traits of the feminine character as did satirists. Nor did he pay attention to anthropological problems like those which came to be increasingly pondered by scholasticism. Bernard thought of woman's position solely as it related to the only thing which interested him: the salvation of the whole human race. Andrew the Chaplain, the troubadours, and other writers despised women either because they considered themselves, as males, to be superior to her socially, or else because they saw in her a means of satisfying their pleasure or the object of ill-repressed lust or again because they were 'philosophers' in the style of John of Salisbury. To find out whether John despised women in real life as vehemently as he makes out in his *Polycraticus*, we would need to examine his correspondence. An outstanding humanist, he was very probably quite different at heart than he showed himself in his literary works.[56]

---

[55] This presupposes the typology of twelfth-century theologians, as treated and justified in 'Renewal of Theology', in *The Renaissance of the Twelfth Century*, ed. Benson G. Constable (Cambridge, Mass., 1981).

[56] Let us simply note the fact that the volume of more than 800 pages mentioned in note 318, above, has no letters to women. In contrast to Bernard, John of Salisbury wrote about them and against them, but not to them.

Each had his own literature. Bernard's was the literature of a theologian. As such, he esteemed woman as the creature and image of God as highly as man. Capable of sharing the same salvation as man and, moreover, able to contribute outstandingly to the work of the Saviour in the Mother of God, she is a model of many virtues, the instrument of admirable works, a symbol of the Church and of the soul united to God.

Woman is part of humanity. Antifeminism is antihumanism. In the Middle Ages, such an attitude could be excused by the literary tradition shackling many writers but one to which Bernard owed nothing. One of his statements, *Ego humanum non nego*, 'I deny nothing human', has been compared to the famous verse of Terence, *Homo sum, humani nil a ne alienum puto*, 'I am a man; nothing human is foreign to me'.[57] Bernard's humanism was certainly limited by his ambient culture. We cannot reproach him for not sharing the culture of later ages. Nor can we reproach him with antifeminism because he was courageous enough to keep himself free from an attitude deeply rooted in contemporary literary tradition.

<hr>

[57]The rapprochement has been made by C. Mohrmann, '*Observations sur la langue et le style de saint Bernard*', in *SBOp* II (Rome, 1958), *Introduction*, p. xxxiii.

# EPILOGUE

## 1. *From Bernard to Pseudo-Bernard.*

AN UNBIASED READING of all Bernard's texts makes it
evident that he was not antifeminist. We even may
get the uneasy feeling that we ought to apologize
for having gone through so long an enquiry simply to
perceive so obvious a fact. This research was worth doing,
however, because certain texts which Bernard did not compose have called up the most adamant reproach about his
so-called misogyny, a reproach which lingers on even in
our own day. That someone should want to prove that
even John of Salisbury was not the woman-hater his letters
would lead us to think is proof enough that concepts like
antifeminism and misogyny are relative. We may even
come to wonder whether it is legitimate to use such language, for it inevitably simplifies mind-sets which are both
complex and charged with meaning.

Here we have been considering only Saint Bernard.
Similar research ought to be carried out on other monastic
authors before we tax them with these same attitudes. At
least Saint Bernard's originality is fully highlighted when
he is compared with what has been said by obscure anonymous writers who either placed their writings under his
name or had them attributed to him by others. An apocryphal, long-unedited, letter which has been unearthed,

159

allows us better to evaluate, by way of contrast, what Bernard really thought.[1]

This letter is a typical and extreme example of an anti-feminist current which existed in the twelfth and thirteenth centuries in various circles: orthodox, 'catharist', monastic, clerical and lay, religious and courtly. This text offers the advantage—if we may say so—of being more explicit and better developed than many others and it gathers in a single page quotations and ideas strewn about in other works. Moreover, the context shows the real meaning of the stand it takes against woman, in connection with women: it warns monks and clerics against sexual relations which they have by their profession sworn to abstain from. A preoccupation of this kind justifies to some extent the intentions behind such works, even if it does not excuse all the means to this end. Yet it does not excuse leaving aside an entire part of the message handed down by tradition. For example, in the text under consideration, there is no mention of the Mother of God. And everything ancient profane literature, Holy Scripture, the Fathers of the Church, and medieval texts and examples had handed down about the role women played in history is ignored. On the other hand, we do find literary themes taken from Stoics and satirists from Hesiod to Juvenal and Seneca, via the *Sentences* attributed to Secundus, Appius' book on the *War of Hannibal*. The result is an invective of rare violence and one which, as one historian has acknowledged, betrays Saint Bernard's thought.[2]

## 2. *The Uniqueness of Saint Bernard.*

Several pseudo-Bernards were monks, sometimes belonging to the same Order he did and almost his contem-

---

[1]'Un témoin de l'antiféminisme au Moyen Age', in *Revue bénédictine* 80 (1970) 304–309.

[2]M.T. d'Alverny, 'Comment les théologiens et les philosophes voient les femmes', in *Cahiers de civilisation médiévale* 20 (1971) 118, no. 83.

poraries. So he is not representative of all monks, even though he testifies to certain inclinations and attitudes common to many. But Bernard is the most outstanding, and soars above them. He stands in a class by himself, not only in comparison with minor and often anonymous authors, but also with those who, after him, are the most eminent. What has been said already about his sources, sources common to his circles, does not explain everything. We still have to discern what it was that, in the field under discussion here, makes him not only original but even unique.

Certainly his exceptional literary genius is itself enough to tell us that he would not stoop to the satire of women that filled so many school copybooks and to which everyone—even some of the masters—tried his hardest to add new features, pleasant or ridiculous, simply copying them from ancient authors, or from Saint Jerome, and modifying as he wanted. There is a level of vulgarity to which Bernard never sank. What astonishes us about him, when we compare him to others and to the pseudo-Bernards, is his discretion, his restraint, in a word, his good taste. He might be violent, but he was never virulent. He never gave in to facile insult. Many of the details he used to denounce vice, for example, came from the delicate mind and worthy doctor Saint Ambrose,[3] and others copied him without any hesitation.[4] Geoffrey of Auxerre, Bernard's conscientious secretary, set down in writing the exhortations his abbot made to the clerics of the Rhineland. Allusions to the frivolity of certain men and women is immediately balanced by a reference to the qualities of both, beginning with the 'modesty and reserve of women, and all that this sex exhausts itself in bearing'.[5] Bernard was fair to everyone.

---

[3] *De officiis ministrorum*, I.I, c.77–78; *PL* 16:46.
[4] John of Fruttuaria (Pseudo-Bernard), *De ordine vitae*, 8; *PL* 184:565.
[5] *De colloquio Simonis cum Jesu*, 9–10; *PL* 184:442.

The liturgy maintained in the Church a spiritual and doctrinal tradition which never condemned or underestimated woman indiscriminately. The texts, it is true, varied. A writer acquainted with the use made of the Old Testament in English, says, 'Woman's role is never systematically curtailed; on the contrary', and goes on to add, 'There is no victory for Deborah', who 'had a good role'. And Dalilah who urged Samson to sin 'is not in the least passed over'.[6] It was not always and everywhere the same. The possibility existed of modifying the dose, as it were, of the feminine models held out by the liturgy for imitation or reproach. On the whole, however, a positive point of view dominated, and this fact had its influence on Bernard.

One might object that all clerics took part in the liturgy and received from it their greatest—perhaps their only—biblical training on womankind, as on everything else. But this did not prevent John of Salisbury and other writers from being misogynists. True enough. But it is one thing to take part in the liturgy out of obligation while spending the rest of one's time in intellectual, pastoral, or worldly pursuits, and quite another to make the liturgy, the Church's own prayer, the centre of one's life, and to feed one's piety at its table and have no other source of joy, as is the case in monastic life. This difference of circumstances alone is enough to let us distinguish the theology of the cloister from the theology of the schools and clerics in general, a distinction which holds true in the field of spirituality as well. It explains those shades of meaning and tone which we notice in devotion, in deep psychological and spiritual attitudes. For John of Salisbury, the liturgical Bible was one among many sources of knowledge. For Bernard it was the principal, practically the only, daily food for thought.

---

[6]M.M. Lares, 'Types et optiques de traductions et adaptations de l'Ancien Testament en anglais du haut Moyen Age', in *The Bible and Medieval Culture*, edd. W. Loerdaux -D. Verhelst (Louvain, 1979).

Bernard not only took in the message of the liturgy. He also helped form its making in and for his own milieu, and in this way he revealed some of his own personal bents. When the cistercian liturgical books were being reformed, he introduced significant changes, in particular in connection with the veneration to be paid to holy women.[7] For example, he composed an entirely new office for the feast of Saint Mary Magdalene. Texts about her already existed, but they were dispersed throughout the liturgical cycle, especially at Eastertide. He collated and organized these texts into a completely new collection centered on Mary Magdalene, the apostle of the resurrection. He also introduced into the offices for the feasts of the Virgin Mary many responsories composed of verses from the Song of Songs.[8] In one of his *Sermons on the Song of Songs* we find an example of the deep impression made on him by the *Lives* of holy women which inspired traditional liturgical repertories. In this sermon Bernard speaks of the nobility which is ours by nature (*naturae ingenuitas*) and by which we exist as the image of God and resemble him as members of his family.[9] The liturgy for the feast of Saint Agatha contains two antiphons inspired by her legend: She answers her judges with the following words 'I am indeed noble (*ingenua sum*) and I belong to a respectable family, but our greatest nobility (*summa ingenuitas*) is manifested in the service of Christ.[10] Though this sort of text tells us probably very little about Bernard's attitude to women, it does show the extent of the influence he received from the liturgy, including celebrations for holy women.

---

[7] I am grateful to Fr Chrysogonus Waddell of Gethsemani Abbey, for having given me information he is preparing to publish.

[8] *Monks and Love in Twelfth Century France*, 38–40.

[9] SC 83.I; II:299,3.

[10] The legend of Saint Agatha, given in the first two antiphons of Vigils for her feast, February 5.

Biblical tradition is the privileged source for christian thinkers, who receive its ideas and images through various channels. Bernard had a personal way of assimilating and collating them into an original synthesis in a manner uniquely his own. And it is there that we find the only worthwhile explanation of his distinctiveness in his teaching on women as on every other subject. He was gifted with an absolutely exceptional ability to situate any detail in the general framework of the history of salvation, that is, of the revelation of the mystery of Christ. All that Bernard thought or experienced was for him only part of a reality of cosmic dimensions. He, like every theologian or any cultured person worthy of the name, achieved the ultimate moment when he experienced the mass of individual details and elements of information, as part of an organic whole, part of a plan coextensive with the totality of revelation., It was no longer a matter of detached morsels of truth, particles in juxtaposition yet retaining their individuality. Bernard had acquired a unifying insight into the total mystery of Christ. And it was from the standpoint of this fundamental attitude that he understood womankind and women, mankind and men, and everything else.

Take, for example, his amazing insight into the mystery of Israel. We could make a list of anti-semitic passages in which he says practically the same things his contemporaries did. But in telling the archbishop of Mainz about the part the Jews would have to play in the final consummation of the Church, he soars far above any such biassed opinions.[11] But this text is surpassed by his seventy-ninth Sermon on the Song, where we find an astonishing passage in which the Church, because of her immense charity, realizes that she will find no satisfaction until the Synagogue becomes the Bride of Christ she herself is.[12] Bernard's ability to situate the Jews in the total flow of the history of

---

[11]Ep 365.2; VII:321,15–322,1.
[12]SC 79.5–6; II:275–276.

salvation explains his greater 'tolerance' than that of the great-hearted Peter the Venerable. Peter wanted to finance the crusade by confiscating the Jews' goods. Bernard thought it sufficient to deprive them of the excessive interest they took on loans.

Elsewhere, in Sermon 83, Bernard sketches what is surely the most pessimistic picture of our human condition.[13] But in the same paragraph he stresses the fact that, though 'we be damned and despairing', we have every reason to await not only forgiveness, but even marital union, the highest intimacy a soul can possibly attain with the Word. If Bernard could say something like that, it was because he set everything contingent and concrete within the perspective of the whole.

Another, equally symbolical, example, though its historical nature cannot be proved, is the story told in the *Fourth Life* of Saint Bernard. John the Hermit describes him polishing his shoes with his brothers and chatting with them. Along comes Satan, disguised as a black monk, and reproaches Bernard for not having a servant do this dirty job for him. Bernard answers that he has never had servants, only sons. And then he goes on to make an astonishing profession of faith for the demon to hear: it is not right that a being created for the highest bliss and for beauty should clean the shoes of a being who is but dust and ashes.[14] What reverence for creation! Even in Lucifer Bernard respects God's work. This is only possible for a person who has an integral experience, a panoramic view of revelation as a whole. It is easy to see how he was able to regard women as something other and better than seductresses of Adam and his like.

Elsewhere, the *Exordium Magnum* shows us Bernard scolding his monks as only he knew how to do. Then suddenly 'completely aflame with the spirit of brotherly

---

[13]SC 83.I; II:298–299.

[14]*Vita quarta*, II.16; *PL* 185:549.

love', he assures them they need not be discouraged, however guilty they may be and however great their sins, if only they believe that the depths of the Lord's mercy are limitless: even Judas would be full of hope if he were here in the school of Christ's charity, sharing this form of life.[15] With what great joy Bernard sees Constantius, once a robber, a seducer, and a murderer, become a model of lay brothers. He goes so far as to clothe him in his own tunic in one of those prophetic gestures of which he was so much the master.[16]

In brief, even though Bernard may have shared the anti-feminist tendencies of his contemporaries, he also saw that the role women played at every stage of sacred history was part of the total mystery of Christ. Womankind may bear the mark of her mother Eve, but she also foretells and anticipates the glory of the Bride without stain or wrinkle. Likewise, if Bernard happens to point out that women have faults—something he rarely does— he more often suggests that men are no better. His prejudices are the same for both sexes. And though he may at times seem pessimistic, he always ends on a note of optimism.

Furthermore, the profound understanding he had of the lowly aspect of the mystery of Redemption determined his attitude to the 'weaker sex'. One of the major themes of classical liturgy is that woman, though frail by nature in comparison, is just as capable of heroism as man. God takes pleasure in everything that is poor in this world. If women are poor by nature, then by that very fact they are all the more apt for salvation, more than men with their natural strength, self-assertiveness, and spirit of domination.

Finally, the mystical and theological tradition in which Bernard moved certainly developed within him the most

---

[15] Conrad of Eberbach, *Exordium magnum Cisterciense*, Dist. II.5, ed. B. Griesser (Rome, 1961) 101.

[16] *Ibid.*, 15, p. 109.

profound respect for women. He often refers to the Church as the Body of Christ, but he considered the Bride the most appropriate symbol for the Church. His entire ecclesiology is centered on this paradigm. And his favorite image for speaking of the relationship between the individual and the Word, Christ, is that of Bride and Bridegroom.

This all helps us see why Bernard always treated women with as much respect as he did men, and why he did not hesitate to speak of God in both the feminine and the masculine. He was secure enough within himself and even-handed enough theologically to be able to speak and to write to women, and about womankind and women, with honest openness, and without being in any way inhibited by some deformity that led him to antifeminism. Any personal tendency he might have had to misogyny immediately found a corrective in Scripture and the liturgy. On the other hand, had he had any such abnormal leaning, Bernard would have found, in these same sources, texts and pretexts to justify his deviation. The texts of the liturgy alone would account for nothing, were it not for Bernard's genius for synthesis and balance, which allowed him to profit by everything without getting bogged down in detail and to maintain a universal perspective. John of Salisbury and others had the same texts Bernard did, but they received them with minds already conditioned by earlier prejudices drawn from other sources.

Bernard's attitude to the feminine was strongly marked by the liturgy, or rather by the liturgical life, not on account of this or that specific text about womankind, but because the Bible and the liturgy together kept him in a state of constant awareness of the totality of the mystery of Christ. In this context he pondered the feminine with the same clarity he did everything else. The technique of patristic and medieval exegesis made the task easier: each text, interpreted according to the different senses of Scripture, was an opportunity for bringing together in a single panoramic view, and fusing into a unified experience, the historical past, reality present in the sacrament, and future consummation. For Bernard, an individual woman was not only herself but also a sacrament—in the broad and ancient sense of the word—of the eternal Woman: Eve before the fall, Eve after the fall, the bride of the Song of Songs, Mary, the Church, the bride without stain or wrinkle, the harlot of Babylon, the woman clothed with the sun. Narrower minds chose one or another of these different aspects and gave it undue stress. Bernard took them all, for they are all various and complementary aspects of a mystery which is too broad, too full for us to reduce it to any single one of them.

# EXCURSUS

T WELVE TIMES IN ALL his works Bernard uses the diminutive *muliercula*, whereas he makes some three hundred uses of *mulier*. *Muliercula* means literally 'little woman'. What did Bernard really intend to say when he used this word? Normally the meaning varied according to the context.

A recent lexicon of medieval Latin distinguishes five different meanings: the first is simply 'woman' with an affective nuance: we find this note of tenderness when the word is applied to the Virgin Mary, for example. Then the meanings vary: weak woman, feeble female, fallen woman, low-born woman, or peasant, and, lastly, 'good woman'.[1]

We find all these meanings in Bernard's works, in phrases which show the extent of his mastery of Latin and of the delicate shades of meaning he was able to give the words he used.

It is certainly the 'weak woman', the object of a great love, who was intended in the short Parable of a sermon on the Song (65.4; II:174, 27), where human nature in its sinful

---

[1] *Novum glossarium mediae latinitatis*: *M-N*, ed. F. Blatt (Copenhagen, 1959) col. 895.

condition, its lowliness, is compared to a poor little creature to whom God, in his love, stoops down like 'a very tall
giant'. The same contrast is seen between 'Dame Will' who
in Saint Peter, despite her power for self-mastery, obeys
the voice of an ordinary woman and denies knowing Christ
(Gra 39; III:194, 14). We find an overtone of compassion
again in letter 62 (VII; 155, 10) for a 'poor woman whom
Satan had for many years tied up in many and tangled
knots of sin'. Now freed, she is like a 'little lamb looking for
a shepherd', like the lost sheep of the Gospel (Lk 13:16).
Bernard begs the bishop of Verdun to help her. It should be
noticed that here we have the only text where there is a
connection between Satan and an individual woman, not
womankind in general. And Bernard does not say that she
is a creature of Satan, but that she has set herself free from
him and thus returned to her normal state. Lastly, in the
*Life of Saint Malachy* (45; III:350,16) we read that this bishop
expelled a demon from a woman who, because of this
possession, had become 'deserving of pity'.

The sense of 'a fallen woman' seems to be found in three
texts in which Bernard reproaches his monks (Miss IV.10;
IV:56,13; Ep 2.11; VII:21, 24) and bishops (Ep 42.4; VII:l04,
11) for competing with *mulierculae* by their elegance and fine
clothes. In these three texts the pejorative sense of the
word is applied to men, indeed to ecclesiastics.

When denouncing the Rhineland heretics, Bernard used
the word to speak of those women with whom the heretics
'shut themselves up' in their hiding places, or with whom
they live in unlawful cohabitation, and to whom they
preach their doctrine. The meaning is clarified by the context: these *mulierculae* are illiterate peasant women—
*rusticae et idiotae*—who were easily led astray in their ignorance.

In letter 404 written to the recluse Albert (VIII:285, 7), the
sense of the word is not clear. Bernard tells Albert that he is
not to receive the visits of *mulierculae*, or to converse with
them. This could mean all sorts of 'women'—as he writes a

little further on in his letter—who want to come to chat with a hermit.

Finally, one sentence merits special attention because in it Bernard warns a cardinal of the danger of the discussions—in the specific sense which the word *disputationes* then had in the schools—which Abelard is supposed to have had 'in the streets and the public places'. There he 'discusses the catholic faith' and the profound mysteries of salvation (Ep 332; VIII:271,14–15). A few lines before, Bernard had written 'He discusses with children, converses with *mulierculae*'. The context would make it seem that Bernard had in mind people who by reason of their age or lowly condition lack the culture and necessary preparation to handle subtle questions about sacred teaching.

# TABLE OF ABBREVIATIONS
## OF THE WORKS
## OF SAINT BERNARD

| | |
|---|---|
| Abb | Sermo ad abbates |
| Abael | Epistola in erroribus Abaelardi |
| Adv | Sermo in adventu domini |
| And | Sermo in natali sancti Andreae |
| Ann | Sermo in annuntiatione dominica |
| Apo | Apologia ad Guillelmum abbatem |
| Asc | Sermo in ascensione Domini |
| Asspt | Sermo in assumptione B.V.M. |
| Bapt | Epistola de baptismo |
| Ben | Sermo in natali sancti Benedicti |
| Circ | Sermo in circumcisione domini |
| Clem | Sermo in natali sancti Clementis |
| Conv | Sermo de conversione ad clericos |
| Csi | De consideratione libri v |
| Ded | Sermo in dedicatione ecclesiae |
| Dil | Liber de diligendo deo |
| Div | Sermones de diversis |
| Epi | Sermo in epiphania domini |
| Ept Mal | Epitaphium sancti Malachiae |
| Gra | Liber de gratia et libero arbitrio |
| IV HM | Sermo in feria iv hebdomadae sanctae |
| V HM | Sermo in cena domini |
| Hmn Mal | Hymnus de sancto Malachiae |
| Hum | Liber de gradibus humilitatis et superbiae |

| | |
|---|---|
| Humb | Sermo in obitu Domni Humberti |
| Innoc | Sermo in festivitatibus sancti Stephani, sancti Ioannis et sanctorum Innocentium |
| JB | Sermo in nativitate sancti Ioannis Baptistae |
| Mal | Sermo in transitu sancti Malachiae episcopi |
| Mart | Sermo in festivitate sancti Martini episcopi |
| Mich | Sermo in festo sancti Michaëlis |
| Miss | Hom. super *missus est* in laudibus Virginis Matris |
| Mor | Ep. de moribus et officiis episcoporum |
| Nat | Sermo in nativitate domini |
| Nat BVM | Sermo in nativitate B.V.M. |
| I Nov | Sermo in dominica I novembris |
| O Epi | Sermo in octava epiphania domini |
| O Asspt | Sermo dominica infra octavam assumptionis |
| O Pasc | Sermo in octava Paschae |
| OS | Sermo in festivitate Omnium Sanctorum |
| Of Vict | Officium de sancto Victore |
| Palm | Sermo in ramis palmarum |
| Par | Parabolae |
| Pasc | Sermo in die Paschae |
| Pr Ant | Prologus in Antiphonarium |
| p Epi | Sermo in dominica I post octavam Epiphaniae |
| Pent | Sermo in die sancto pentecostes |
| Pl | Sermo in conversione sancti Pauli |
| Pre | Liber de praecepto et dispensatione |
| IV p P | Sermo in dominica quarta post Pentecosten |
| VI p P | Sermo in dominica sexta post Pentecosten |
| PP | Sermo in festo SS. Apostolorum Petri et Pauli |
| Pur | Sermo in purificatione B.V.M. |
| QH | Sermo super psalmum Qui habitat |

| | |
|---|---|
| Quad | Sermo in Quadragesima |
| Rog | Sermo in rogationibus |
| SC | Sermo super Cantica canticorum |
| I Sent | Sententiae: PL 183: 747–58 |
| II Sent | Sententiae: PL 184: 1135–56 |
| Sept | Sermo in Septuagesima |
| Tpl | Liber ad milites templi (De laude novae militiae) |
| V And | Sermo in vigilia sancti Andreae |
| V Mal | Vita sancti Malachiae |
| V Nat | Sermo in vigilia nativitatis domini |
| V PP | Sermo in vigilia apostolorum Petri et Pauli |

# CISTERCIAN PUBLICATIONS INC.

## Kalamazoo, Michigan

## TITLES LISTING

### THE CISTERCIAN FATHERS SERIES

## Texts and Studies
## in the
## Monastic Tradition

# THE CISTERCIAN STUDIES SERIES

\* *Temporarily out of print*          † *Forthcoming*

Saint Gregory Nazianzen: Selected Poems

Eight Chapters on Perfection and Angel's Song
(Walter Hilton)

Creative Suffering (Iulia de Beausobre)

Bringing Forth Christ. Five Feasts of the Child
Jesus (St Bonaventure)

Gentleness in St John of the Cross

*Distributed in North America only for Fairacres Press.*

## DISTRIBUTED BOOKS

St Benedict: Man with An Idea (Melbourne Studies)

The Spirit of Simplicity

Benedict's Disciples (David Hugh Farmer)

The Emperor's Monk: A Contemporary Life of
Benedict of Aniane

A Guide to Cistercian Scholarship (2nd ed.)

*North American customers may order
through booksellers or directly from
the publisher:*

Cistercian Publications
St Joseph's Abbey
Spencer, Massachusetts   01562
(508) 885-7011

Cistercian Publications
Editorial Offices
WMU Station
Kalamazoo, Michigan   49008
(616) 387-5090

*A complete catalogue of texts-in-
translation and studies on early,
medieval, and modern Christian
monasticism is available at no
cost from Cistercian Publications.*

*Cistercian monks and nuns have been
living lives of prayer & praise, meditation
& manual labor since the twelfth century.
They are part of an unbroken tradition
which extends back to the fourth century
and which continues today in the Catholic
church, the Orthodox churches, the
Anglican communion, and most recently,
in the Protestant churches.*

*Share their way of life and their search for
God by reading Cistercian Publications.*